My Children's Heritage

My Children's Heritage

Answers to Your Questions About Life, Happiness, and Holiness

L. H. Houston

Millennium III Publishers
SIMPSONVILLE, SOUTH CAROLINA
2007

My Children's Heritage
Answers to Your Questions About Life, Happiness, and Holiness
Copyright © 2007
by L. H. Houston

ISBN 0-9625220-8-2

Published by
Millennium III Publishers
P.O. Box 928
Simpsonville, SC 29681

Unless otherwise noted, all Scripture quotations are from the New King James or King James versions of the Bible.

All rights reserved. Except for traditional dialogue or scholarly criticism, no portion of this book, electronic or otherwise, may be reproduced without written permission of the publisher.

Contents

Foreword	vii
About the Author	ix
Introduction	1
1 : Grace	7
2 : Why Study the Bible?	15
3 : The Ten Commandments	25
4 : The Holiness Code	43
5 : Jesus, Our Role Model	59
6 : The Pauline Epistles: The Heart of New Testament Sanctification	69
7 : Prayer	85
8 : Major Contemporary Issues	99
9 : Forgiveness: For Growth and a Free Mind	127
10 : The Principle of Giving	143
11 : Your Heritage	153

Foreword

In the eyes of the world today a heritage or legacy is often thought of as fame and fortune, an empire built to last generations. Seldom does one think of instructions on what it means to be a Christian as a heritage. To those who love the Lord what better legacy to leave than to make sure your children, grandchildren, and future descendants understand what and in whom you believe, what you stand for and how to accomplish that for themselves.

I didn't understand until I became involved in the lay witness program how many churches are filled with Christians who don't know how to be a Christian. As Lee states, "Many Christians never get past accepting justification." They have accepted God's prevenient grace and His justifying grace and there they stand.

They do not know or realize what a rich, full, blessed, and power-filled life is available to them.

No one had taught me how to be a Christian and to grow into sanctification until a lay witness team showed me what I was missing.

I can remember my father teaching me most of these points about the law when I was young. I thought I was the only one whose father taught them not to use the term liar loosely. Father taught me many other bible principles. Many of these teachings came back to me as I read this manuscript. My father didn't explain in depth as Lee has how the laws and the Ten Commandments, handed down from God, affect our lives and the society around us. I accepted what my father told me just because he was my father, and I knew what he stood for. Those who read the essays in *My Children's Heritage* will have a better understanding of why we should and shouldn't do some things.

Although the foundation laid by my father was a good one and I accepted Christ, I knew there was something missing, there had to be more. I was searching when I attended a lay witness mission at our church. The leader of that mission saw that I was searching and led me onto the path of sanctification. I am ever thankful to them. Those who read *My Children's Heritage* will have their eyes and spirits opened and they will be thankful to Lee for this opening.

In the short time I have known Lee I have admired his intellect and his thirst for knowledge. I think he has learned his lessons well. He has created a lasting legacy for future generations, tempered with love. Just as our Father is love.

As you read this, feel the spirit urging you to believe in His prevenient grace, to be justified in His grace, and grow into sanctification.

Your brother in Christ,
Garry C. Boyette

About the Author

Lee Houston is a Christian layman and businessperson who began his business career at the age of 14 and worked his way up corporate structures to become president of three companies. He has also served on numerous boards, run his own consulting business, and traveled to twenty-one countries. Additionally, Lee has been on staff at North Carolina State University, as well as having taught ad hoc at two smaller colleges. A Methodist Lay Speaker with a Master's degree in communication, Lee has addressed many churches, civic, and business groups. He is a Purple Heart veteran.

Originally written as a gift to his children and grandchildren, *My Children's Heritage* stresses the need for Christians to follow the path of sanctification as well as to answer some of the questions addressed to Lee by audiences over the years.

Lee has grown in his search for what he calls, "the narrow path." He considers himself an orthodox Christian who believes absolutely in the grace of God and that faith is the only way salvation can be received. However, he believes too many Christians stop their spiritual growth after they accept Christ, never to go on to the difficult duties and rewards of Christian sanctification.

I dedicate this book to my other half,
Judy Dunn Houston,
as a gift to Courtenay, Lee III, and Sarah.
In loving memory of Oliver Blackstock, the finest man I ever met.

Introduction

You must make your choice.
Either this man was, and is, the Son of God:
or else a madman or something worse.
You can shut Him up for a fool,
you can spit at Him and kill Him as a demon;
or you can fall at His feet
and call Him Lord and God.
But let us not come with any patronizing nonsense
about His being a great human teacher.
He has not left that open to us. He did not intend to.
— C. S. Lewis

Like any parent, when I die I want to leave my children something of significant value. This gift must be something they cannot lose, that thieves cannot steal, and that will not rot or decline in value (Matthew 6:19-21). When I die, the only thing I have that meets these criteria is the kind of wisdom that comes from my traditions, my heritage.

My heritage is the Christian faith. I want to make sure my children understand this heritage well, for this heritage is under siege. America is losing its life, its soul, its Christian faith. The Christian faith is being ignored, attacked, and abandoned – not only in practice but also in theory, directly and explicitly, by those who mold our children's minds – by our secular educational, entertainment, and media establishments.

How America Has Changed

In America today, arguments that are rational, traditional, and valid often fall on ears deafened by prejudice, passion, ignorance, misunderstanding, incomprehension, and ideology. It is not intellectually fashionable to believe in Christ as anything more than a human teacher. Rather, we Americans love peer acceptance, approval and support. We fear non-conformity, eccentricity, and not being part of the in-crowd even when the in-crowd looks increasingly like garbage swirling around in a cesspool. I am writing down my heritage because I want my children and grandchildren to have an in-depth understanding of why I believe in Christ, my Christian heritage.

America was once the home of religious tolerance. That has changed. America now has a new religion. It is the equality of all faiths. The notion that Christ alone is God – superior, authoritative, supernatural – violates this equality. Many Americans believe any religion that contains much great and good wisdom is acceptable, equal. To them, the idea that Christ's teachings and person are far greater than Buddha's or Mohammad's is immoral, even dangerous. This new ethic invites each person do that which seems right in his or her eyes. It teaches that all moral laws are man-made and therefore can be unmade by man. This religion of equality is a wide easy road to travel (Matthew 7:13-14). Equality of religions makes no demand on us to be discriminating, to choose a religion and justify that choice. It tolerates, nay encourages, the denial of ethical distinction. Equality of religions requires that we must be nonjudgmental.

Would we really want God to be "nonjudgmental" and not root out all sin? Would we want salvation to mean only salvation from punishment and not from sin? Would we want God to tolerate sin in heaven too? Would we want everyone to bring all of their earthly bad habits to heaven, everything from dishonest politicians and pornography to stealing and adultery? Would we really want a heaven that needed police and lawyers?

How Churches Have Changed

Further, my heritage is under siege from within the church by modernism. Modernists interpret the Bible and cardinal elements of the Gospels as myth – neither literally true nor literally false, but spiritually or symbolically true. This is the standard line of liberal theology departments in many colleges. Modernists interpret everything – or at least everything miraculous, supernatural, or morally unpopular – figuratively or non-literally. They insist on an unbelieving, skeptical attitude toward the Bible. Modernists wish the Scriptures would answer less loudly, less clearly, more subtly so that only a scholar could properly interpret them. That would give them a more worldly importance. God did not design the Bible to be a dark puzzle for bright scholars but to be a bright lamp for common travelers through a dark world.

Modernists read their philosophy of naturalism into the Bible. They read miracles out of the Bible not because the text tells them to but because their philosophy tells them to. Historians tell us that the closer a source is to the event it describes, the more likely it is to be reliable. Yet, modernists assume that the message of Jesus was misunderstood by Christ's own disciples, by their disciples and by nearly all Christians for many centuries until the modernists finally deciphered it. Modernists have undermined faith more effectively than atheists have. These wolves in sheep's clothing have misled many more sheep than the honest wolves, secular humanists, have.

Christianity cannot rid itself of its founder's claim to be the only Savior without ceasing to be Christianity. Passages such as Romans 1 and John 1:19 tell us that God shines light into everyone's mind, and speaks to all people through conscience. Christians do not claim to know how many people respond to this knowledge of God in such a way as to be saved, but they do claim that Christ said He was the only way. There is only one straight gate, one narrow way that explains living the Sermon on the Mount. Yes, "Jesus only" is terribly narrow (John 14:6). Nevertheless, there is only one correct way to accomplish many worthwhile things.

What the secularists and the modernists do not believe is the logic of it all. To live like evil people is to succumb to evil, to become evil, but to hate evil people is also to succumb to evil. Hating evil people makes it impossible to avoid pharisaic self-righteousness or to hate sin without hating sinners (Leviticus 19:17). The truth is, to hate anyone at all is to become hard, dark, and negative.

Jesus' simple answer was repentance and forgiveness. Forgiveness neither condemns nor condones (Matthew 5:45-48). It admits evil is evil; it does not say, with the blind indifference of pop psychology, "There is nothing to forgive." God's forgiveness dissolves the glue between the sinner and the sin and sets the sinner free. Repentance does the same thing from the side of the sinner, because forgiveness is God's response to the sinner's repentance. Repentance and forgiveness will work together to make the world into the Garden of Eden God intended it to be.

The Core of My Christian Heritage

Now that I have briefly described my view of the world in which I write *My Children's Heritage*, I must now tell you that the core of my Christian heritage is the grace of Christ. For me, understanding His grace is easiest when broken into three parts: 1) prevenient grace, 2) justification through faith in Christ, and 3) living in the grace of Christ, or personal sanctification.

When we are born, we are born into sin (Romans 5:12). However, we are born with God's grace and love readily available. This is God's prevenient grace. It exists before we are even aware of it. God is always with us. "... He causes His sun to rise on the evil and the good, and sends rain on the righteous and the unrighteous" (Matthew 5:45). We may not know it, or we may reject it and rebel against God. However, God continues to work in our lives to bring us into a right relationship with Him.

Acts 16:30-31 tells us how to have this right relationship with

Introduction

God: The jailer "brought them out, and said, Sirs, what must I do to be saved? And they said, Believe on the Lord Jesus Christ, and thou shalt be saved, and thy house." When we receive God's grace by believing that His Son died for our sins, we are justified by faith and regenerated through His saving grace.

The Upward Calling: Philippians 3:14

Many Christians never get past the initial justification. However, justification is intended to be a starting point in one's walk with Christ: "... go and sin no more" (John 8:10-12). The walk with Christ is called sanctification. Sanctification is living for God's purpose, it is obedience to the principles of the law, the Sermon on the Mount, and Paul's teaching on sanctification. Sanctification is a Christian's growing emancipation from evil, a Christian's growing good works. Sanctification is growing toward the fulfilling of the first commandment in the Bible, to have dominion over the earth (Genesis 1:28), and it is growing toward the fulfilling of the Great Commission to make disciples of all nations teaching them to observe all Christ commanded of us (Matthew 28:18-20).

The part of Christ's grace I wish now to pass along to my children is beyond prevenient grace, beyond justification, for my children have all accepted Christ by faith. Because of Christ, they are declared righteous (Romans 4:6, 8-10). Therefore, while I want to write about justification, what I want to leave my children is an in-depth understanding of that next step, growth in grace – sanctification. If I could give my children a book that explains this growing process, I would accomplish half of my goal. *My Children's Heritage* is a book I wrote to make sure my children and grandchildren would continue to be exposed to the truths of sanctification long after I have died.

Paul, in Philippians 3:12-15 and in Romans 7:12-25, says that works are not the basis of salvation, but that good works necessarily flow from salvation. Therefore, *My Children's Heritage* has to include some of my works, the many times I have stood before an audience and answered questions about the Bible. My calling has caused me to meet people pastors rarely see, people who have no understanding of Christianity, even some people who are anti-

Christian. Yet, when I speak to these people, be it a civic group or a business group or in private conversation, they asked similar questions: How do you know there is a God? I am a good person; I feel like a just God will send me to heaven. What is grace? Then there are contemporary issues such as homosexuality and abortion; what do the Scriptures say? People are amazed that the Bible has answers to all of these questions. *My Children's Heritage* is a book I wrote to make sure my children will be able to answer these same questions. Answering these questions is the other half of the book.

The first chapter of the book explains salvation by grace. The second chapter, Why Study the Bible?, takes its direction from 1 Peter 2:2 and Ephesians 4:11-15. These verses say that we must learn the Word and grow in the Bible's knowledge, in order to be more Christlike. Then we begin the study of the law with Chapter 3, The Ten Commandments. In Chapter 4 I talk about The Holiness Code or the six hundred and three other laws of the Pentateuch. These laws are God's gift, our Father's gift, to His children. These rules are to help us know the personal growth Paul writes about in 1 Thessalonians 4:1-7. These are the directions we are to follow until completely putting off the "old man" and putting on the "new man" (Ephesians 4:22-32; Colossians 3:5-16; Galatians 5:13-26). Personal sanctification is the beginning of a life-time process, a vital element in the New Covenant described in Hebrews 8:10, "For this is the covenant that I will make with the House of Israel after those days, says the Lord: I will put my laws in their minds, and I will write them on their hearts. I will be their God, and they will be my people." This is the goal of sanctification.

The balance of the book answers many of the questions I have been asked over the years. These chapters are roughly grouped by subject matter, and do not necessarily have to be read in order. Overall, the book's ultimate goal is to show that if we all were saved by grace through faith in Christ and then faithfully sought personal sanctification, the world would become a virtual Garden of Eden. It would be the blessed society which is envisioned in the Sermon on the Mount.

1 : Grace

The gods we worship write their names on our faces,
    be sure of that.
And we will worship something –
    have no doubt of that either.
We may think that our tribute is paid in secret
    in the dark recesses of the heart –
        but it is out.
That which dominates our imagination and our thoughts
    will determine our life and character.
Therefore it behooves us to be careful
    what we are worshipping,
for what we are worshipping we are becoming.

— Ralph Waldo Emerson

In the Introduction, I discussed why I have written this book and what I hope it accomplishes. Now, I must lay the foundation with a discussion of salvation by grace through repentance and faith, resulting in regeneration and justification and how these things should lead to sanctification.

I will start by describing how my Mother came to salvation. Like many modern Americans, she sought God intellectually. Her experience had elements in common with what Paul described in his experience at Mars Hill – how he approached the unbelieving Athenian intellectuals (Acts 17:16-34).

"The Greeks Seek After Wisdom"

In his address to the pagans, Paul first challenged their mental capacities. He began with their altar to the unknown god to show them logically that this unknown god was really the one and only true God. My Mother was fascinated with this same kind of logical thinking. Her favorite Scripture was Matthew 22:37-38: "Jesus said, 'You shall love the Lord your God with all your heart, with all your soul, and with all your mind.' This is the first and great commandment."

My Mother, like the Greeks, sought God via her "mind." I remember my many long conversations with Mother; the logic and common sense that the Scriptures contained had to be beyond human abilities to construct. That was the bait that kept her constantly searching for that glimpse of God that she was only able to catch a few months before her death. It was only in those last few months that she realized that her heart and soul had not been involved, but that they must be. Mother found faith. It was only then that she knew she was one with God's love. It was only then that she experienced grace. These thoughts guided me as I wrote this book.

I know that some who read this book might be atheist or agnostic. Others, though they may well be churchgoers, would have little knowledge of the Scriptures. I knew that exposing people to the beauty, logic and the practicality of living by God's law has always been a lure with which to catch unbelievers. God's law and Christ's principles make absolute sense. They provide an understanding of life and of the world not found in the writings of the finest philosophers or history's greatest thinkers. Even though the Scripture says, "by the deeds of the law no flesh will be justified in His sight" (Romans 3:20), still, exposing people to God's law makes them think that maybe there is something to Christianity.

"What purpose then does the law serve?"

This knowledge eventually accomplishes something even

more important than an appreciation of the logic of the law. In Romans 3:19, Romans 7:7-13 and Galatians 3:19-26 Paul tells us that the purpose of the law is to show us that we are all guilty of sin so that we may turn to Christ in repentance and faith. Our minds can use the law to recognize the fact that sin reduces personal happiness and prevents human societies from living at peace. However, the impossibility of following the law shows us that sin is so much a part of human existence that we cannot rid ourselves of it. We are human. It is dishonest to assume we can do well at keeping the Ten Commandments let alone all six-hundred-thirteen biblical laws. "As it is written: 'There is none righteous, no, not one'" (Romans 3:10).

Frankly, even if we were good, it would not be enough to enter into God's perfect presence. If we who wish to keep the laws cannot, what hope is there for a world full of people who are primarily interested only in their own comfort? If we do not have the power to keep the law, how do we ever stand a chance of surviving, of finding peace as brothers and sisters in this age of weapons with the power to wipe us off the face of the earth?

The Gospel: The Power of God Unto Salvation

The answer: God has the power. Indeed, only God has that power. As creatures, we are extremely limited. Our free will is a gift so powerful that it is easily misused. The Bible proposes a remedy for this state of affairs – the grace of God. Men and women's self-efforts will not enable them to escape from self-centeredness. Self-effort alone is not enough and leads only to death. The self must be lured out of its anxieties and hostilities into communion with God. Only His infinite love, working at the deepest levels of our human nature, can perform this seemingly impossible task. The message of the Gospels is that infinite love has manifested itself in Jesus, He is calling men and women back to the communion God intended the day He put Adam and Eve in the Garden. The cross is the symbol of the utter selflessness and self-giving character of His divine love – *agape*. Only this grace is sufficient to heal humanity's broken nature.

Our minds let us see how much sense this answer makes. But,

the mind is not enough. Faith is required. Grace can only be born where one enters openly and completely into salvation disregarding costs.

Grace is Christ forgiving those who condemned Him to that most painful of all tortures, being hung from a cross, suspended only by His nail torn flesh, until dead. Only the sea of God's grace has the power to change the selfish human soul. Only by grace is a person transformed, not of his or her own power, but by a gift from Almighty God.

We find grace and faith a part of the life of every character in the Bible who found favor with God. We see Abraham was honored by the grace of God for his faith: "And he believed in the LORD, and He accounted it to him for righteousness" (Genesis 15:6).

The great king David said, "Behold, I was brought forth in iniquity, And in sin my mother conceived me" (Psalms 51:5). Yet, David's faith made him special to God.

Jeremiah said, "The heart is deceitful above all things, And desperately wicked; Who can know it?...Heal me, O LORD, and I shall be healed; Save me, and I shall be saved, For You are my praise" (17:9, 14).

And Paul concludes, "...through one man sin entered the world, and death through sin, and thus death spread to all men, because all sinned...through one man's offense judgment came to all men, resulting in condemnation, even so through one Man's righteous act the free gift came to all men, resulting in justification of life" (Romans 5:12, 18).

It took only one act, Adam's sin, to pollute the world. It took only one act, the perfect life of Christ, to eradicate that sin. Adam was made perfect but earned death by committing one sin. Christ was made perfect but gave Himself to death for sinners, though He had no sin.

The righteous God sentenced Adam while sinful humankind sentenced Christ. Yet, Christ asks His Father, while hanging on the cross in awesome pain, to forgive sinful humankind. His Father honored His request. Though we deserved death, the fate of Sodom and Gomorrah, for God to give us what we deserved would have been to dishonor an appeal of the Son. Christ died to save us from our sins. God honored Christ's righteousness and His sacrifice.

And now Christ can faithfully promise, "Most assuredly, I say to you, he who hears My word and believes in Him who sent Me has everlasting life, and shall not come into judgment, but has passed from death into life" (John 5:24).

God gives us free will, and it takes one act from us to join the fold: believing in Christ as Savior, making Him the center of our lives. Repentance and faith involve accepting God's grace and rejecting our own selfish desires. Faith also accepts the responsibility of being a child of God. While Paul used logic on Mars Hill to get people's attention, he knew that ultimately people must trust God's grace – each person, individually, by his or her own choice.

Paul said,

> For Christ did not send me to baptize, but to preach the gospel, not with wisdom of words, lest the cross of Christ should be made of no effect. For the message of the cross is foolishness to those who are perishing, but to us who are being saved it is the power of God...but we preach Christ crucified, to the Jews a stumbling block and to the Greeks foolishness (I Corinthians 1:17-18, 23).

The message is simple: God in His infinite love saves as many folks as will trust Him. The result is justification and regeneration.

The purpose of Christ's coming was not to judge the world but to save the world. This salvation is a gift. Further, this gift is more wonderful than just a happier life. The gift includes eternal life: "These things I have written to you who believe in the name of the Son of God, that you may know that you have eternal life ...." (I John 5:13).

Many people accept the gift of eternal life and stop; their growth ends there. It is as if once saved they disregard Christ's instructions and are simply waiting for the rapture. That is not what the Bible tells us to do to realize the fullness of the gift. We find fullness as we obey:

> Go therefore and make disciples of all the nations, baptizing them in the name of the Father and of the Son and of the Holy Spirit, teaching

them to observe all things that I have commanded you; and lo, I am with you always, even to the end of the age (Matthew 28:19).

After regeneration, 1) we have a new "heart" (Ezekiel. 36:26-27); 2) are a "new creation" (2 Corinthians. 5:17-19); 3) are a "new man" (Ephesians 4:24, Colossians 3:10); and 4) have the "divine nature" (1 Peter 1:4). Only then are we able or willing to grow in personal sanctification.

The work and the wonders are just beginning. We are to spread the Good News, to change the world into a better place. The work of spreading the Gospel requires full maturity. As we spread His New Covenant message others are saved and the result is a new and better world.

Jeremiah wrote,

> But this is the covenant that I will make with the house of Israel after those days, says the LORD: I will put My law in their minds, and write it on their hearts; and I will be their God, and they shall be My people (31:33).

It is this new covenant imprinted on the hearts of Christians that drives them into the world forsaking self, having gained the infinite forgiveness necessary to demonstrate love so plainly that even the most hardened sinner knows that these people are special. These saved people go about doing good works and sharing the Gospel's message as the results of this grace placed deep within their hearts. It is by their unselfish works, their selfless lives, that they preach the Gospel unto the ends of the earth.

Christian work is a part of grace called sanctification. "But to all who believe Him and accept Him, He gave the right to become children of God" (John 1:12). Children do their Father's will; they help Him with His work. The book of James, often misunderstood, discusses this:

> What does it profit, my brethren, if someone says he has faith but does not have works? Can faith save him? If a brother or sister is naked and destitute of daily food, and one of you says to them, "Depart in peace, be warmed and filled," but you do not give them the things which are needed for the body, what does it profit? (James 2:14-16).

Does that spread God's love? Does that spread God's word? James continues, "Thus also faith by itself, if it does not have works, is dead" (James 2:17). Sanctification includes doing God's work. Sanctified Christians "go and make disciples of all nations." Our job as saved people is to do that which He has equipped us to do.

> And He Himself gave some to be apostles, some prophets, some evangelists, and some pastors and teachers, for the equipping of the saints for the work of ministry, for the edifying of the body of Christ, till we all come to the unity of the faith and of the knowledge of the Son of God, to a perfect man, to the measure of the stature of the fullness of Christ (Ephesians 4:11-13).

God has equipped us. So great is the amount of work to be done that we never have to worry about being unemployed. Much of the world has not yet been touched by Christ's church.

That is our job. Luke's parable pictures God as the waiting father of a boy who has left home and wasted his substance in riotous living (15:11-32). Jesus likens Himself to a shepherd who leaves the sheep that are safe in the fold, and goes into the wilderness to find the lost (John 10:1-16). Can we follow Him in this unselfish work?

> Let nothing be done through selfish ambition or conceit, but in lowliness of mind let each esteem others better than himself. Let each of you look out not only for his own interests, but also for the interests of others (Philippians 2:3-4).

So many Christians go to church on Sunday and that is where it ends. We are to share the joy of saving others, of seeing the world move a little closer to being the Garden of Eden God intended us to inhabit. Christians change the world. This is real joy!

The message of this portion of this book is simple: By faith we receive the grace of Christ, and His grace brings salvation. But, that is just the beginning! Jesus broke down barriers that separate people. We are to continue that work. Reach for the joy of a life dedicated totally to Christ's work! Do not be just another Sunday-morning Christian. Change the world! Whether you are a pastor, a mother, an engineer, a garbage collector, or a factory worker, show the world by the quality of your work that you are a child of God, a changed person. Again, James challenges us; can we show our faith without works? But he says, "I will show you my faith by my works" (2:18).

We must humbly and unselfishly serve those in need whether by simply listening attentively to a fellow worker's problems in the office or by giving money discreetly to someone in need. That is what Christ would do. Follow the Lord in difficult matters as well as in things you find agreeable; that's where the joy is.

2 : Why Study the Bible?

Jesus ... is easily the dominant figure in history.
Now it is interesting and significant,
  isn't it,
that a historian, setting forth in that spirit,
without any theological bias whatever,
should find that he simply cannot portray
  the progress of humanity honestly
without giving the foremost place
  to a penniless teacher from Nazareth.
  — H. G. Wells

Moses was old. His life's goal was almost accomplished. Only the Jordan River separated him from the Promised Land, yet he would not be going over. But the people of his nation would be going over. They were carrying God's two greatest gifts to humanity: the promise of a coming redeemer, and the law from the lips of God.

Moses, under God, had fathered a nation. Now Moses would speak his last words to his children. These last words must have been a terribly emotional and important time for Moses and for the nation. So, what did Moses say? "Hear, O Israel, the statutes and judgments which I speak in your hearing today, that you may learn them and be careful to observe them" (Deuteronomy 5:1). Then Moses followed with a review of the Ten Commandments.

Further along in the Bible we find David, Israel's greatest King, saying, "It is good for me that I have been afflicted, That I may learn Your statutes. The law of Your mouth is better to me Than thousands of coins of gold and silver" (Psalms 119:71-72). Jesus said, "Take my yoke upon you and learn from Me, for I am gentle and lowly in heart, and you will find rest for your soul" (Matthew 11:29). If Moses said learn God's laws, if David said, learn God's statutes, and if Christ calls on us to learn from Him, how can we do less than study at their feet?

Bible Study and Western Culture

Studying is obviously a prerequisite and must be a constant companion of the growing Christian – the Christian whose foundation is the "solid rock" – the Christian who can weather the storm and be there to lead others when the storm passes.

Today's widespread lack of Bible study among Christians, even among Christian leaders, prompted me to write this book for my children. Our secular world has swept many Christians into one of those junctions in history where people have discovered the almost rightness of a great deal that is wrong and the almost wrongness of a great deal that is right. Many highly educated and sophisticated people have little knowledge of God or what the Bible factually says. People who have PhD's in difficult-to-master subjects often could not pass the final exam to graduate kindergarten when it comes to Christianity.

If the Bible teaches us values and orientation in life, if the knowledge of God's teachings is the foundation on which all else rests, then no human pursuit could be more important than the study of His teachings.

Essential to Education. Bible study tells us much about what makes up our culture. Many people have gotten upset because "the courts have taken prayer out of schools." It's much worse; in some areas of the country leaders have over-reacted to court rulings and have taken education out. I would think that this would upset even the secular world. No one has said much.

At the top of this chapter, I quoted the famous historian, H. G. Wells, saying that he "cannot portray the progress of humanity honestly without giving the foremost place to" Jesus. The history of Western civilization, its towering figures and economic progress, are not understandable without a decent knowledge of Christianity. Understanding Dr. Martin Luther King's last speech in Memphis without an understanding of the Pentateuch is impossible. One must look in the Bible to know what motivated people like John Brown to rebel against slavery. The Mayflower Compact, forerunner of our Constitution, and the Pilgrims' first Thanksgiving came directly from biblical ideas and rules. The comprehension of the works of Joan of Arc, Handel, Dante, and on-and-on-and-on is hopeless without understanding Western religious teachings.

Heavily affected by Christianity are our government, economy, family life, ethics, philosophy, art, and science. Understanding Christianity is essential to a good education and as enduring as any science, art, or literature. No education can be complete without some detailed understanding of the Bible.

Moral Emancipation. Furthermore, study is the forerunner to proper behavior. If in the twenty-first century we must spend years-upon-years in school to be successful in a technological world, it is wise to spend a portion of those years involved in God's Word so that we have a base. I say education, as distinguished from training, because education aims at emancipation of the human being.

Education vs. Training. Training is what happens in many schools today as we turn out consumers, automatons, for our materialistically driven world. Knowledge of God provides an opportunity to realize genuine human existence. God's teachings outlive graduation from college or even graduate school. The principles, concepts and values found in the Bible long endure after all the technical information in our heads is obsolete. Being educated in Godly matters makes us more than human in a biological sense;

through it we comprehend the essence of our humanity – as one made in God's image.

Being truly educated means finding some ground for personal existence and for authentic social relationships with other persons that go beyond mere externals and manipulation. If human beings are more than animals, God's teachings make the difference.

A Study of Ultimates

Paul is correct, "...we cannot do anything against the truth, but only for truth" (II Corinthians. 13:8). Genuine Bible study is a disciplined dialogue concerning ultimates. True study turns its back on narrowness and dogmatism as contradictions of the Bible's true spirit. True study recognizes the difference between indoctrination and investigation. Investigation must regulate the study of God and His law. The Bible provides us with the knowledge we need to spot idolatries, false teachings, what we can and cannot trust. Bible study provides us with a way to examine our society, our government, our world, and ourselves. Bible study prepares us to recognize honest dialogue of good will among men and women who differ in their faiths. God created all men and women in His image and for His purpose. Therefore, points of view that differ from our own must be worthy of study and discussion as we each weigh our respective opinions against God's immutable standard.

Clear Vision. Beyond this, as I have already intimated, Christianity is the realm of the ultimately true and supremely valuable. Bible study is the power to plunge into the depths of existence and discover new dimensions of meaning. Study reveals what is most important and most exciting in life: God is! He exists! And, because He exists, all else exists. Studying God is studying what differentiates us from the beast in us: His Image!

I hear people describe something exciting as "making them high." If one could compare being high on drugs to the riches of the Bible, it would be like comparing one's view of the world from the depths of a closed grave to one's view of the world from a mountaintop on a pristine day in June. There you can see forever. God is. Again, studying God is studying what differentiates the great in us from the beast in us.

2 : Why Study the Bible?

The Vision Grows Dim. Things have changed. When I was a boy, the Ten Commandments were highly visible and taught in most schools. Guns and ammunition, even dynamite, were readily available at the local hardware store, but no one ever thought about taking them to school. We did not view the Commandments as religious dogma but as absolutes, minimums, for decent behavior. That, of course, has changed and changed dramatically.

The Morning News

One must ask if the news I watched this morning is the product of a society that has lost its absolutes, its minimal standards of behavior. On the news, a judge sentenced a thirteen-year-old boy to twenty-eight years in prison for shooting his teacher between the eyes. The District Attorney who had brought the boy to trial and had won a conviction for murder was now considering charging him with perjury for attempting to get another youth to lie for him on the stand.

There was another child in the news. This one charged with murdering a friend while practicing wrestling moves on him. Psychologists tell us that the psychological effect of watching carefully scripted wrestling on television is identical to the psychological effect experienced by Romans watching gladiators fight to the death or watching criminals burn on a stake.

There was more on the news: A mayor of a large American city, the father of two teenaged girls, was charged with paying a lady so that he could have sex with the lady's young daughter. And even as I write these lines, there is still in the news a congressman who has had numerous affairs with young women.

Is this the kind of world in which we want to live?

Sin: A Reproach to Any People

In the 1990's a President humiliated Americans by blatantly lying about adulterous affairs, and then questioned our intelligence with statements like, "It depends on what your definition of 'is' is."

Latch key children come home to tune-in to television programs that make the abnormal and abhorrent seem normal. Let's see...there was the mother who was having sex with her daughter's boyfriend; there was the girl who tried to, and still wanted to, murder her mother; and there was the fifteen-year-old girl who had sex with at least fifty-four men and boys.

Is this the kind of world in which we want to live?

This country is indebted to that pious and noble organization, the ACLU, for a modicum of effort protective of free speech. However, in recent years the actions of the ACLU seem dedicated to the eradication of our county's Christian heritage, our history. How can an organization, once dedicated to the protection of free speech, now be its enemy? What is so terrible about the Ten Commandments that we must remove them from schools and courtrooms? With so many violations of free speech rights in government and industry, why isn't the ACLU busy with projects that are more substantial? If a school identifies the Commandments as Jewish and Christian dogma, then they are educational. The Ten Commandments are important historical documents for many reasons including having been the basis of the codes of law in most western countries. Our laws certainly incorporate them. These attacks by the ACLU are more than illogical; they are absurd.

Is this the kind of world in which we want to live?

What I have been pointing out, and there are innumerable examples, is how nonsensical our world has become as it has drifted away from God's teachings.

A Code to Live By. One of the primary reasons for studying the Bible, particularly the Pentateuch, is that it gives us a code to live by. A code tested and proved by millions upon millions of people. The law is simple, it is logical, applicable to all of life's circumstances. It is a code that not only consistently keeps people out of trouble; it maximizes individual and societal happiness.

High Cost of Lying. Consider the ninth Commandment, "thou shalt not bear false witness." Lies have become a part of American society; however, there has been a predictable cost. The tobacco companies continued to claim that nicotine was not addictive, and people have become more cynical of big business as the result. Journalists who have political agendas and who have fabricated stories make us more suspicious of the media. Environmentalists who have made exaggerated claims have had the same effect on an otherwise worthy cause. Then there are the politicians.... There is nothing moral or Godly about lying. Given the consequences you would think that more business people would challenge the tobacco companies, more journalists would demand truth, more environmentalists would sound off about poor science and that voters would reelect fewer scoundrels.

The Scourge of Adultery. Then there is the law against adultery. Watching prime-time television could well lead one to believe that infidelity is America's latest sports craze. Our principles, if they are worthwhile, permeate our entire being as the Scriptures advocate. Our principles should be so much a part of us that they reach into our private lives, our kitchens, our workplaces, and even our bedrooms.

I am not saying that there are things that are not private; there certainly are. However, we should discipline our passions, for by being able to control them we are able to achieve the kind of discipline that serves our lives well. Morphine and other drugs administered by a doctor to someone in pain are a blessing; but they are poison to an addict. Sex is similar. In marriage sex is a gift; out of wedlock it is a sin. The marriage relationship should be so special that no person has the audacity to break it.

By placing adultery between murder and stealing in the Ten Commandments, God seems to be saying that, if we cross this boundary of intimacy, we are destroying something more sacred than property rights, something almost as sacred as human life. We are destroying society. Entire communities are in poverty because adultery has caused the break-up of families. Adultery is not a victimless crime; it is a horrible betrayal.

How about the children of divorce? We must recognize that illicit sexual intimacy is fraught with danger, and pregnancy is possible; we need the marriage boundary. God commands that we control our sexual appetites, channel our desires into appropriate relationships, and preserve the locus of safe human intimacy.

God blessed marriage where a husband and wife become "one flesh." When marriage moves beyond a mere biological function into a sacred relationship, individuals and the whole society are happier. Our children have homes that permit them the opportunity to grow up in a controlled way.

This law, like all of God's laws, has practical as well as moral consequences. Should we trust a politician who has committed adultery – who has broken a vow to his or her spouse and does not mind lying about it?

Defeating Destructive Behavior. Study of the Bible begins proper action. Think about the times when you have broken the laws of God and remember the pain you suffered. Why repeat hard lessons we should have learned? There is little doubt that the Ten Commandments and the rest of God's law let us lead lives that are far more apt to be happy and productive.

This is never more true than in a crisis or when under pressure. In a crisis there is no time to study or deliberate; we must be able to choose proper behavior instantly. Our Christian obligation is to study God's Word so that we know right from wrong spontaneously, without hesitation. The Bible is humankind's best friend.

Teach Diligently. Further, our obligation extends to teaching God's Word to our children in some format that goes beyond a few bedtime Bible stories. Few learning endeavors produce results effortlessly; we must make an effort. Obtaining intellectual satisfaction and competence will require you to invest a great deal of time.

You may seek out a "crash course" in Bible studies. These can help overcome fears and stimulate interest. They can provide a fundamental knowledge substructure. Nevertheless, knowledge and intimacy in God's Word are the products of ongoing, concentrated effort, years and even decades of training, repetitive endeavors, and hard work. I have found studying the Bible to be one of life's greatest pleasures. I recommend it to anyone who enjoys a challenge.

The third Commandment says that we should not swear falsely, not take God's name in vain – there is no worse way to break that Commandment than to publicly proclaim to be a Christian while privately relegating Bible study to simply reading our Sunday school lesson. It is time for Christians to make a commitment to Bible study, to understanding and practicing God's law. There are no shortcuts. True biblical insight begins with hard work and deep study.

3 : The Ten Commandments

> *Never will there be found a precept comparable*
> *or preferable to these [Ten] commands,*
> *for they are so sublime*
> *that no man could attain them by his own power.*
> – Martin Luther

This chapter concerns the heart of God's law, the Ten Commandments – awesome in holiness, powerful tools for living a happy life. They provide a great personal blessing and advantage for those who understand and follow the commandments. They are a large part of the base, the firm foundation our children need if they are to lead productive lives in this time of rampant sin. For those reasons I will discuss them in some detail. However, to avoid confusion, I want to talk briefly about salvation. This is necessary before we focus on the study of these beautiful words, as we journey down sanctification's pathway.

A Brief Explanation

I write emphatically that keeping the law does not save the soul. The Apostle Paul said it best: "Therefore by the deeds of the law there shall no flesh be justified in His sight..." (Romans 3:20). In another context, Paul said, "For by grace you have been saved through faith, and that not of yourselves; it is the gift of God, not of works, lest anyone should boast" (Ephesians 2:8-9). This is an elementary doctrine: obeying the law, virtuous works, or good deeds do not save.

Yet, the Bible clearly instructs us to follow the law.

Why?

Paul asked and answered the same question: "What purpose does the law serve?" (Galatians 3:19). He answered in Galatians chapters 3 and 4 and Romans chapters 3 through 8. Paul says that God gave the law for two reasons: The first is to bless us, that we, His Children, may live happy, peaceful, and fruitful lives. The second is to show us how sinful we are that we may turn to Christ for salvation, for "...by the law is the knowledge of sin" (Romans 3:20).

Then Paul explains this in more detail:

> What shall we say then? Is the law sin? Certainly not! On the contrary, I would not have known sin except through the law. For I would not have known covetousness unless the law had said, 'You shall not covet....' And the commandment, which was to bring life, I found to bring death. For sin, taking occasion by the commandment, deceived me, and by it killed me. Therefore the law is holy, and the commandments holy and just and good. Has then what is good become death to me? Certainly not! But sin, that it might appear sin, was producing death in me through what is good, so that sin through the commandment might become exceedingly sinful (Romans 7:10-13).

When a person, therefore, sees himself or herself as "exceedingly sinful," he or she may then turn to Christ for forgiveness. A true believer then is not under the law (Romans 6:14) as in the Old (Mosaic) Covenant but under the New Covenant: "This is the covenant that I will make with them after those days, says the Lord: I will put My laws into their hearts, and in their minds I will write them" (Hebrews 10:16, also see 8:7-13, Jeremiah 31:31 and

33). Under the New Covenant, the heart is made receptive to God's laws; and as we study them they are written in our minds as well, ready to bless us with happiness, joy, and wellbeing in a thousand ways. Keeping the laws and commandments of God is thus seen not as the cause of salvation but the result.

In summary, salvation is wholly by God's grace, not by the law. Yet, the Bible clearly instructs us to follow God's law. Again, why? I believe the law is God's loving gift to His children. For me and many others seeking sanctification, following His law maximizes our happiness, the power of our existence, and thus the happiness of human kind. Yet, few Christians study God's law in detail, daily. It shows our society is slipping further from God's law, slipping at an ever-increasing rate.

The Law: A Code to Live By

Jesus emphatically instructs us to follow God's law:

> Not everyone who says to Me, 'Lord, Lord,' shall enter the kingdom of heaven, but he who does the will of My Father in heaven (Matthew 7:21).

> Do not think that I came to destroy the Law or the Prophets. I did not come to destroy but to fulfill. For assuredly, I say to you, till heaven and earth pass away, one jot or one tittle will by no means pass from the law till all is fulfilled (Matthew 5:17-18).

At Mount Sinai, God gave Moses 613 laws. We know that He singled out ten of them for special treatment. We know this in two ways. Firstly, God wrote these Ten on two stone tablets, handed them to Moses, and Moses' copy of them was kept in the Ark of the Covenant. Secondly, the accounts in Exodus Chapters 19 and 20 strongly suggest that God initially spoke these directly to the people – not relaying them through Moses as He did the other laws.

As one studies Christ's teachings, He tightens the practice of the law with nine of the Ten Commandments. Only in the law concerning the Sabbath did Christ loosen the practices of the Jews of the first century. Christ was a Jew. He perfectly kept not only the Ten Commandments, He followed all of God's laws. Yet, few

Christians know about the 613 laws contained in the Bible. Indeed, not many Christians pay much attention to the Ten Commandments. This clearly contrasts with Christ's teachings. This is not the path to the abundant life God promises, the path of sanctification.

So why is obeying God's law important? Obeying God's law is not about getting into Heaven; grace does that. Obeying God's law is about honoring God and leading a happy earthly life.

In Numbers 15:39, God says we are to follow His law "so that you do not follow your heart and eyes in your lustful urge." In Deuteronomy 10:12, 13 God tells us that He wants us to keep His law "for your good." In John 10:10 Jesus says, "...I am come that they might have life, and that they might have it more abundantly." In Matthew 6:10, Jesus teaches us to pray that God's will, His law, should be done here on earth as it is already done in the happiest place of all, heaven. "Thy kingdom come, thy will be done in earth, as it is in heaven." Obeying God's law is about God's love for us, our happiness, and His glory.

Focus on the Decalogue

In this chapter, I will concentrate on the Ten Commandments while using some of the information from the other 603 laws to expound. I am going to use a different order from the normal start at the top and come down.

The Sabbath: A Day to Heal the Heart. I will first look at a commandment that today we give only lip service to, the Fourth Commandment:

> Remember the Sabbath day, to keep it holy. Six days you shall labor and do all your work, but the seventh day is the Sabbath of the LORD your God. In it you shall do no work (Exodus 20:8-10).

The reason I cover this Commandment first is that I want to demonstrate what a better world this would be, what a higher quality of life we would lead, if we did keep this Commandment.

Before I discuss the benefits of the Sabbath, which actually means rest, I quote Jesus, "The Sabbath was made for man, and not man for the Sabbath. Therefore the Son of Man is also Lord of the Sabbath" (Mark 2:27, 28). Here Christ is clearly interpreting the law for a Christian application while maintaining the underlying spirit of the law.

Underlying the spirit of the Sabbath is the radical notion that human beings have worth even when they are not working. Rich or poor, we are alike on the Sabbath. Many in our society take this notion of rest too far. We forget that while the Sabbath is a day of rest, its ultimate goal is holiness.

Much to Learn. We Christians have much to learn from the Jews. I have read a number of accounts of holocaust survivors telling what sustained them through their time in those Nazis hells, concentration camps. Scores of Jews were comforted during their ordeals by their memories of Sabbath day celebrations. No matter how poor, they remembered how they stopped work on the eve of a Sabbath, put on their best clothes and ate the best meal of the week. Even the poorest saved all week to have a plentiful meal that night. The meal was a joyous celebration. They walked to the synagogue to remember and study the righteousness of the Lord. The day of the Sabbath was a happy time full of family and laughter. These wonderful memories sustained countless Jews during their suffering at Dachau, Auschwitz, Buchenwald and the many death factories. No greater gift can a parent give a child than such wonderful memories.

A Time to Celebrate. The Sabbath is for the building of the spiritual element of the family, for resting the body and the mind away from the burdens of life. It is a time to celebrate the kind of happy life God wanted us to have when He placed us in the Garden of Eden. The commandment is about promoting the happiness of the family, a pleasurable cheerful time spent in the home enjoying our loved ones. The Sabbath is a time to put away all of our cares, toils, grief and sorrow. Songs are to accompany dinner. Anyone who has had the opportunity of knowing the inner life of a family that observes the law of the Sabbath with strictness felt astonished at the wealth of joyfulness, gratitude, and sunshine witnessed. The law enriches the home that celebrates and hallows the Sabbath.

Living Below Our Privilege. It's the Twenty-First Century and many have forgotten these joys. In this era, few people seem to realize how empowering a loving family is to its children. Imagine if every family in this country spent the Sabbath enjoying each other, laughing, worshipping, and sharing God's law and love. Children raised in such a loving environment rarely become less than the best they can be. A better place this world would be if we all made obeying the spirit of the Fourth Commandment a personal goal. God's law is logical. It is about our happiness. It is about societal happiness.

The Sabbath is not an interlude. It is a climax. It is about time and not space. It is a sanctuary in time. It is about connecting with what matters. The Sabbath is to be our time to connect with God. If you want to experience something of spiritual existence, of the world to come, sanctify the Sabbath.

Please note, the other six days of the week are for work, "Six days you shall labor and do all your work...." Work is also a blessed part of the law.

Parents: Where it All Begins

The Fifth Commandment ties directly to the Fourth; indeed the Fifth Commandment ties our duties to God into our duties to each other. In Matthew 22:35-40 we find these words:

> [A Pharisee] asked [Jesus] a question ... saying, "Teacher, which is the great commandment in the law?" Jesus said to him, "'You shall love the LORD your God with all your heart, with all your soul, and with all your mind.' This is the first and great commandment. And the second is like it: 'You shall love your neighbor as yourself.'. On these two commandments hang all the Law and the Prophets."

The Tie that Binds. The first four of the Ten Commandments (having no other gods, no graven image, not taking God's name in vain and observing the Sabbath) address our relationship with God, that is, "Thou shalt love the Lord thy God." The last five of the Ten Commandments (concerning murder, adultery, theft, lying and covetousness) address our relationship with our fellow human beings. That is "Thou shalt love thy neighbor as thyself."

The Fifth Commandment ties these nine Commandments together. Exodus 20:12, "Honor your father and your mother, that your days may be long upon the land which the Lord your God is giving you." This Commandment is the link between our duties to God and our duties to each other.

Why? Because, this is where it all begins! Sin is rebellion against God's authority, and rebellion is usually also against what our parents taught us. Sin is dishonoring God and thus dishonoring our parents. That is, God has placed sons and daughters under the tutelage of the parents. Parents are the vice-regents of God.

Parents must teach children how to live, how to get along with others, and about the character and will of God. Parents are responsible for teaching children about God's rules for happy living. The Fifth Commandment shows us that, in our children's eyes, parents stand in the place of God. The Fifth Commandment recognizes that there are three partners to the creation of a human being – mother, father, and God.

Honor: A Term of Tribute. Twice mentioned in the Old Testament and six times mentioned in the New Testament, the Fifth Commandment holds a special place in God's rules for our lives. Jesus demonstrates this in Matthew 19:19. "Honor your father and mother. Love your neighbor as yourself." Why does Jesus use the word "honor" in our relationship with our parents and the word "love" when speaking of our relationship to others? Why is it that way throughout the Bible?

"Honor" is not a term of endearment. Rather, "honor" is a term of tribute. Love is the binding attachment for family, for friends and neighbors. Honor is an attribute for deeds of accomplishment, for high positions of authority. The purpose of this wording is to impress upon us the importance of children exhibiting the same kind of honor to parents accorded God. The parents are His representatives for the young in the family.

Role Models of Godliness. Honor does not occur naturally in children. It must be taught. The first time a child wants to do something his or her own way in defiance of his or her parents' wishes, honor must be taught. This is for the good of the child.

A parent's duty is to act in the loving and nurturing ways of God. It is the duty of parents to pass on knowledge, discipline, and respect. Likewise, it is the duty of the children to honor their parents. The greatest achievement open to parents is to be fully worthy of their children's reverence and respect. On the other hand, God promises the children who honor their parents happiness and blessing.

As Go the Parents, So Goes the Nation. Acknowledgement of parental authority reinforces the fabric of human society, makes possible the transmission of values and the progress of humanity. What parents teach their children is the basis on which we build our community relationships. It is upon these community relationships that we build our national relationships. If children do not honor their parents, they will honor no other relationships. If there is not honor in the home, there will be none in our country. If parents do not teach honor of God in the home, our nation will not honor Him. That is why this commandment is important.

Growing Wise at Mom and Dad U. Children are born untrained, blank sheets of paper, unprogrammed computers, little unlearned bundles of joy. Without proper guidance, our sin nature will rule us. Parents have the responsibility not only to teach a child to walk, talk, get an education and so forth; parents also have the responsibility to discipline the child, to teach the child to be Godly. While the child may object to discipline when it is applied, he or she will remember this guidance with fondness when grown.

The result of honoring one's parents is to receive the fulfillment of the promise mentioned in the Fifth Commandment. The Apostle Paul discusses this promise in Ephesians:

> Children, obey your parents in the Lord, for this is right. "Honor your father and mother," which is the first commandment with promise: "that it may be well with you and you may live long on the earth" (6:1-3).

It is the parent's task to lay a firm foundation. Parents set the fundamentals in place for happiness, mental growth, superior habits, and the discipline necessary to prevent a child from having to learn so many things the hard way. Going to the "school of hard knocks" is no fun. Going to the school of parental love and concern is far easier and far more constructive.

The family is the first environment of the child. It is the first school, where we receive our basic education. It is the first church where we learn the foundations of a happy life. The home is the first state in which we participate and learn of law and order.

The home is where we have our first vocation, where we learn to work, where we learn responsibility. The home is the place where the child can make mistakes and experience loving correction. Never again will a person have such a wonderful opportunity. The real world can be a harsh teacher. Paul, in Ephesians 6:1-3, tells us that teaching a child to honor and obey gives him or her the kind of learning experience and discipline necessary to lead a long and fruitful life.

It is a mistake to view civil authority as superior to parental authority when just the opposite is true. The home is where the child learns obedience. Godly parents, even those with little formal education, have the best interest of the child at heart.

Their Greatest Treasure. Parents view a child as the greatest treasure they have. Imagine the change if every parent put their children above all else (excepting only God Himself), treated their children as their greatest treasure, taught them the character and ways of God. Spending time with children would replace the desire to work so that one could buy a new microwave, a high-definition television, or be a multi-car family.

In many families, materialism has replaced the value of the child. Many people will work long hours to have some material thing, but the children they already have are far more valuable than any material item. Children who grow up in loving Christian homes have the foundation necessary for a long happy life. They have the tools necessary to enjoy and make the best of life's challenges.

For example, many non-Christians in our country live in a world that lacks cultural coherence. It is not clear to them what a father's role should be. Indeed, given the number of children born out-of-wedlock, it is obvious that there are many men unwilling to assume the responsibilities of fatherhood. We need to encourage those who accept these responsibilities.

In the Godly home, it is as natural for a man to be a father as it is for eyes to see, ears to hear, or for feet to walk. Fatherhood is the crowning achievement in a Christian man's life. Rich or poor, educated or unlettered, successful fatherhood is the most memorable accomplishment in a man's life. When a father lies on his deathbed, he remembers none of his worldly accomplishments. He thinks not of the shiny new cars he drove, nor the fine homes he lived in, nor the honors he received.

No.

A father remembers nothing with greater fondness than he remembers his children.

Guardian of Marriage and the Home

Another which is given little attention today is the Seventh Commandment: "You shall not commit adultery" (Exodus 20:14). This is a commandment that many not only do not obey, but in America today many even deny its validity or authority. This commandment against infidelity warns husbands and wives alike against profaning the sacred covenant of marriage. It involves the prohibition of immoral speech, immodest conduct, or association with persons who scoff at the sacredness of purity in marriage. This commandment plainly lays out this action not only during marriage but also before marriage. It clearly applies to men and women and to singles as well as married people.

The Jews saw marriage as a process – Mary and Joseph were betrothed for months before their marriage. So cherished was the marriage relationship that a young Jew could not leave his wife even in time of war until the couple celebrated their first full year of marriage. Even to save one's life, adultery was no option. The penalty for breaking this law was death.

Sexual intercourse is a religious act in a holy home. The strict punishments found in the Bible against adultery are there to show us just how important the family is – to the husband and wife, to the children, to civilization, and to God.

Imagine if every father and mother in this country would make it a goal to obey the laws of God: gone would be the pain and anguish of divorce. Gone would be the anguish of the children of broken homes, gone the necessity of dead-beat-dad laws, and gone the anguish of being a slave to bodily passions. God's law has the power to change America into a virtual paradise.

Which is the Greatest Commandment?

Next we will consider the First Commandment:

I am the LORD your God, who brought you out of the land of Egypt, out of the house of bondage. You shall have no other gods before Me (Deuteronomy 5:6-7).

This law first declares that God is. We are to believe in His existence.

"I" means that God is not an impersonal force. God is a person – the source not only of power and life, but of consciousness, personality, moral purpose, and ethical action. "your God" means He is the God, not merely God of past generations but of every individual in every generation. He is the God "who brought you out of the land of Egypt, out of the house of bondage." He chose the nation of Israel, a band of slaves, to be the people through whom He would enlighten the world, to whom He would send the Redeemer. He is the God of freedom. History is one continuous divine revelation.

This Commandment says in effect, "I, God and creator of everything, care enough about each individual to minister even unto the least of you, a bunch of slaves." God was revealing Himself not only to the elite of the world, but also to the lowest. Since that is true, God cares about each of us as individuals. Therefore, God also cares about what we do. We are obligated to behave as a creation of God, as sons and daughters.

"You shall have no other gods before Me." There are no other gods beside God. The fundamental dogma of monotheism is the unity of God. Nothing else shall receive the worship due to Him. Neither angels nor saintly men or women are to receive adoration as divine beings. We are forbidden to pray to anyone but God. This Commandment also forbids belief in evil spirits, witchcraft, and similar evil superstitions. Furthermore, he who believes in God will not put his trust in chance or luck. This lays down the duty of worshiping God alone, and worshiping Him in spirit – not through images.

All Human Life is Created in His Image

This brings me to the next Commandment, the Sixth, "You

shall not murder." God alone gives life. Created "in the image of God," all people have infinite worth. Apart from capital punishment, war or other grave circumstance, God forbids the intentional killing of any human being. To murder another is to extinguish what God created above all other creations. To murder is to extinguish not only that life, but also every life that may have come from that life. To murder is to blaspheme God.

As for capital punishment or war, no country can be a just and a safe place to live unless it upholds the sanctity of life. A nation must be willing to defend a life with a life.

The law carefully distinguishes murder from accidental killing. The law saves the involuntary slayer of another person from vendetta and the horror that vindictive thinking brings to a society. In the law, we find this Commandment expanded to forbid doing anything by which the health and well-being of a fellow human is undermined. Moreover, it forbids the omission of any act by which a fellow human could be saved from peril, distress, or despair.

Also, a child's life is as sacred as that of an adult. This idea was unique to the Jews. In Greece, weak children were exposed – that is, abandoned on a lonely mountain to perish. In Roman society, parents had the right to kill a child they found offensive. The Greeks and Romans regarded the Jewish outrage toward child-murder as a "contemptible prejudice." "It is a crime among the Jews to kill any child," sneered the Roman historian Tacitus. God says murder of anyone for any reason is wrong.

Idols of All Kinds Are Forbidden

The Second Commandment reads, "You shall not make for yourself a carved image – any likeness of anything that is in heaven above, or that is in the earth beneath,...you shall not bow down to them nor serve them...." (Deuteronomy 5:8-9).

We may not worship the one God in the wrong way. God is Spirit. Therefore, it is an egregious sin to worship God under any external form that human hands can fashion. God is a jealous God. God desires to be all in all to His children. He claims an exclusive right to our love and obedience. He hates cruelty and unrighteousness. He loathes impurity and vice. Even as a mother

3 : The Ten Commandments

is jealous of all evil influences that rule her child, He is jealous when idolatry and ungodliness command our allegiance instead of purity and righteousness.

Later in this Commandment we find "...visiting the iniquity of the fathers upon the children to the third and fourth generation..." is easily misunderstood. However, more detail is found in a later chapter:

> The LORD, the LORD God, merciful and gracious, longsuffering, and abounding in goodness and truth, keeping mercy for thousands, forgiving iniquity and transgression and sin, by no means clearing the guilty, visiting the iniquity of the fathers upon the children and the children's children to the third and the fourth generation (Exodus 34:6, 7).

The key to understanding is the phrase, "by no means clearing the guilty...." Because God is so tolerant, "keeping mercy for thousands [of generations]," we often forget that He is not only a God of mercy but also a God of justice. Sin causes people pain. God disciplines those who cause that pain. That is justice.

There are no victimless sins. "Upon the children to the third and fourth generation" means that children may suffer the consequences of their ancestor's sin for three or four generations. The sin is the problem. It will have consequences for the sinning parents and their innocent children. In addition, the children, because of the example set by the parents, are inclined to commit the same sin their parents committed. In His mercy, God will consider those things.

God's Name is Very Special

Obviously akin to the Second Commandment is the Third: "You shall not take the name of the LORD your God in vain, for the LORD will not hold him guiltless who takes His name in vain." The Third Commandment forbids us to dishonor God by invoking His name to attest what is untrue, or by joining His name to anything frivolous or insincere. God is holy and His name is holy. We may not use His name profanely to testify to anything fallacious, insincere or empty. Jesus, in the Sermon on the Mount, said:

> ... you have heard that it was said to those of old, "You shall not swear

falsely, but shall perform your oaths to the Lord." But I say to you, do not swear at all: neither by heaven, for it is God's throne; (Matthew 5:33, 34).

Our courts permit us to simply affirm the truthfulness of what we say, in accordance with the commandment of Jesus:

> Nor shall you swear by your head, because you cannot make one hair white or black. But let your "Yes" be "Yes," and your "No," "No." For whatever is more than these is from the evil one" (Matthew 5:36, 37).

We may not use the name of God in vain or in flippant oaths. Unnecessarily speaking God's name in common conversation is disrespectful, wrong.

Anyone who swears falsely, whether in God's name or not, is committing perjury. To stay away from this egregious sin, the Essenes held that "he who cannot be believed without swearing is already condemned. Let thy yea be yea, and thy nay, nay. To strengthen your promise with a vow shows that something is wrong."

As we have seen, Jesus had a similar view.

It is remarkable how few people show the total respect due God in this most meaningful and yet painless way. To swear using God's name is akin to swearing by one's father's or mother's name, something few would do.

Misleading Our Fellow Human Being

The only proper use of God's name is to invoke His help – "so help me God" – to tell the truth in our testimony in court, to back up our commitment to the Ninth Commandment, "You shall not bear false witness against your neighbor." This Commandment is concerned with wrong inflicted by word of mouth. This prohibition embraces all forms of slander, defamation, and misrepresentation, whether of an individual, a group, a people, a race, or a faith. This Commandment prohibits any words that enable one human being to take advantage of another.

This Commandment prohibits any words that increase the amount of misinformation in the world. When one person bears false witness to another, he misleads that person. He is attacking his or her ability to make sound decisions. In biblical terms, perjury is a very serious offense, which, unless repressed by the severest penalties, will destroy human society.

Many misquote this Commandment and say, "thou shalt not lie," but "thou shalt not bear false witness" is far more encompassing than simply lying. Truthfulness must be moral. It ceases to be truthfulness and becomes an abominable form of lying when used as a tool of revenge or malice. God will not have us use truth maliciously to ruin another person or put someone to open shame. The Bible sees a talebearer as equal to a murderer since lies destroy a most precious possession in life, a person's reputation. "A truth that is told with bad intent beats all the lies you can invent."

"You shall not go about as a talebearer among your people…" (Leviticus 19:16). Bearing "false witness" means that we are not even to repeat unverified information that may get someone in trouble. If you repeat what you do not know to be true, you are a false witness.

I know that in my own career as a professional manager, no bit of advice is as good to take to heart as this. Many times I have had someone convincingly accuse another person only to find upon further investigation that the talebearer was wrong or had an ulterior motive. I have made it a point to handle such information carefully until I can investigate.

I know of no people who have suffered more at the hands of the talebearer than the Jews. I know of few habits that have caused me more personal pain than being the victim of such tactics.

What We Create is Special

We come now to the Eighth Commandment, "You shall not steal." Property represents the fruit of industry and intelligence. When we steal, we are depriving someone of the fruits of their sweat. Any aggression on the property of our neighbor is, therefore, an assault on that person's personality. This Commandment regulates more than direct stealing. It forbids every illegal acquisition of property by cheating, embezzlement, or forgery. Even legal acquisition of property is forbidden if the law is bent. Any transaction that takes advantage of another's ignorance is wrong.

The use of embarrassment to deprive someone of the fruit of their labor is wrong. Property rights are human rights. Let the property of every human being be as precious to you as your own property. That is the meaning of being "my brother's keeper."

The Seed of Sin

Finally, we come to the Tenth Commandment, "You shall not covet.... You shall not crave...." This Commandment goes to the heart of much evil action, unholy instincts, impulses, or predatory desire. The person who does not covet that which is his or her neighbor's will not bear false witness, steal, murder, nor commit adultery. This Commandment is about self-control. Every person has it in their power to determine whether desires are to master them or whether they are to master their desires. Without this discipline, there can be no worthy life. Discipline is the measure of adulthood. True strength is control of one's passions. This commandment is the ideal Commandment with which to introduce the impact of God's law.

> Oh, that they had such a heart in them that they would fear Me and always keep all My commandments, that it might be well with them and with their children forever! (Deuteronomy 5:29).

The Source of Our Values

No book has done more to influence Western civilization than has the Bible. No part of the Bible has done more to influence Western laws, moral and social codes, than the law of Moses. This alone is sufficient reason for any educated person to study and be versed in the Ten Commandments. These brief Commandments cover the whole sphere of the conduct of both our outer actions and our inner thoughts. These laws lay down the fundamentals of not only individual success but of societal success and of national success. Without these laws God's creations here on earth are incomplete, even meaningless. Without them it is probable that humankind would have already destroyed itself. If we do not adhere to them, we will live to see an Armageddon.

God is.

His will is.

He expresses His will for us, His desire for our happiness, in His law.

4 : The Holiness Code

Her ways [the Bible's ways] are pleasant ways,
and all her paths, peaceful.
— Proverbs 3:17

God created us in His image. Sanctification is the process of learning to live that image, of acting like God's children should act. Ultimately, our goal is to be so completely Christlike that Hebrews 8:10 is realized, "...I will put my laws in their minds, and I will write them on their hearts. I will be their God and they will be my people."

A part of realizing God's goal for us comes from studying the Bible, from the understanding that brings. That study should go beyond the Ten Commandments and the Gospels. I believe we need a firm foundation. I believe a part of that foundation is the other 603 laws in the Pentateuch. I once went through several reference Bibles and studied all of the quotes attributed to Jesus. Many things Christ said came from the foundation, the Pentateuch. It is from this foundation that we can interpret or use the Scriptures to solve moral problems, to grow until someday God's law is written in our minds as well as on our hearts.

Your Commandment is Exceedingly Broad

At one time, I thought parts of Exodus and all of Leviticus, Deuteronomy, and Numbers were the dullest, most boring books I had ever read. I had no understanding of those books, the foundation. Then one day while reading a quote from Deuteronomy, something went off in my mind – from then until now the first five books of the Bible have absorbed some of my Bible study each day.

The verse I read that day, the verse that made me a fan of Pentateuch study, was Deuteronomy 22:8, "When you build a new house, you shall make a parapet for your roof, so that you do not bring bloodguilt on your house if anyone should fall from it." I have always been a manager responsible for the productivity, health, and safety of large numbers of people. Here was the Pentateuch saying something that was directly applicable to my job. Further, I suddenly realized that I had often looked to the Bible for simple specific answers to my questions; but the Bible does not always work that way. Sometimes the Bible will answer a question on several levels. Those answers may well cover far more than was apparent at first reading.

The verse in Deuteronomy concerned a mundane detail from everyday life, yet the law about parapets grabbed my own life experience in a real way. The principle implied covered many of my management responsibilities. Most Bible verses have at least two meanings; one is the simple literal meaning and the other the creative outgrowth of the simple into broad and important principles. This verse was but one of many that God uses to give us simple rules that, with study, we can mate together to form a logical whole. This approach enables this one book to cover virtually all of life's situations. This arrangement allows us to extrapolate from the simple literal meaning, to the creative outgrowth, to the logical implications of the broader principles. At each level of understanding, Bible study reveals the appropriate truth, showing God's perfect will for us at the moment of need.

The Simple Meaning. I will show you what I mean. "When you build a new house, you shall make a parapet for your roof, so that you do not bring bloodguilt on your house if anyone should fall from it." The simple meaning: Most houses of ancient Middle

4 : The Holiness Code

Eastern countries had flat roofs. During the day, the roof served as a work area. At night, the roof functioned as a place to sleep. As I understand it, the hot Middle Eastern sun made the roof an ideal place for such activities as drying grain. On warm dry nights, the roof was the coolest place to sleep. The parapets were to prevent people from falling off the roof. The parapet had to be high enough and strong enough to prevent accidents.

The Broad Meaning. This Biblical law had a real and a simple purpose. However, as a professional, this same Scripture had a much deeper, more far-reaching meaning. This Scripture teaches that the person in charge of a property is obligated to remove or make harmless anything that might cause serious injury. God expects us to foresee the injuries that can ensue from our actions and from our passiveness. It was suddenly so plain. We are to build the kind of safe world in which God would have His children live, work and play. The little verse about the parapet is far more important than it first seems.

This verse about the parapet also addresses one of life's biggest questions, from Genesis 4:9, "Am I my brother's keeper?" Only a murderer, like Cain, totally renounces his or her obligations to humankind. We are not to separate ourselves from our community obligations. If our community is in trouble, we are in trouble. I remember a story that went something like this: Some people sitting in a boat observed another passenger begin to bore a hole under his seat.

The other passengers asked, "What are you doing?"

He answered, "I am boring a hole under my own seat."

The other passengers responded in unison. "But the water will come in and drown us all."

We are our brother's keepers. I am responsible for building a parapet on my house, and you are responsible for building a parapet on your house. It is up to each of us to make his or her area of the world as safe as is humanly practical.

This simple verse about the parapet has to do with respect for the inalienable rights of others – a very far-reaching principle. This verse is about moral action. This verse implies a harmonious arrangement of society, through which we may realize the qualities of God's kingdom here on earth. This verse is about acting in a loving way, but it is not complete for it does not include instruction regarding justice.

Those who do not carry out their responsibilities are to receive justice in the form of penalty. "You shall follow what is altogether just..." (Deuteronomy 16:20). The Bible reminds us that justice is strong enough, divine enough, to triumph without resorting to injustice. "Let justice roll down as waters, and righteousness as a mighty stream," cried the Prophet Amos. Justice is not only among the highest ethical qualities humankind can have, it is the basis for many other ethical qualities. Created in the image of God, each human is sacred and of infinite worth. The parapet is to protect that worth. Hence we all are mutually responsible for erecting a parapet. Those who are less fortunate, the poor and the physically unable, are to receive justice in the form of help. Justice is about building the kind of world in which God would have His children live, work, and play.

For me this thought that started with the parapet says, "Do what is right and good in the sight of the Lord" (Deuteronomy 6:18). God's first concern is with a person's decency. So "...walk in the way of goodness, And keep to the paths of righteousness" (Proverbs 2:20). God says we are responsible for our actions.

God says I am to be righteous. Since I am not righteous, God must have given me the ability to grow in righteousness, to seek sanctification. I must have the ability to act mercifully, with loving kindness, and, in doing so, help to bring peace to the world.

Doing what is right means not blaming others. That is the behavior of a child. I am responsible for my actions. While being responsible, I must not be passive when the chance to be helpful presents itself. This is God's law, His will.

After I came to understand the law concerning the parapet, I began studying the other 603 laws in the Pentateuch. Leviticus Chapter 19 sits at the center of these five books. Not only does it revisit most of the Ten Commandments, it also covers enough of the other laws to give a good idea of the depth and absolute beauty of thought revealed in the law. Therefore, we will now turn our attention to Chapter 19.

4 : The Holiness Code

Equality Under the Law

Chapter 19 begins, "And the LORD spoke to Moses, saying, 'Speak to all the congregation of the children of Israel, and say to them.'" God tells Moses to deliver the law to the entire congregation, and not just to the priests, Aaron and his sons. The idea of equality and fairness under the law, which we now call equal rights, did not start with the Greeks or with Americans. The idea of equality started with God and Israel. At Sinai, God instructed each individual how to lead a happy productive life.

All of God's children are equal. We see as we move through the Bible that it is not enough to act according to the strict letter of the law if such action permits an unfair advantage of one person over another or causes hardship and harshness. Equality requires a higher justice, the spirit of the law. This is implied in the New Covenant which Paul talks about in Hebrew 8:10. It is with this spirit and for this purpose that God instructs us in His law.

Holiness, God's Goal for Us

"You shall be holy, for I the LORD your God am holy" (Leviticus 19:2). Holiness would turn the world back into the Garden of Eden, in which God wanted us to live when He first formed the world. God still wants that for us. Holiness is not a flight from the world into some sort of monk-like renunciation of human relationships. Holiness is fulfilling our obligations to God, to His creation, and to our fellow man.

This thought dominates this chapter of Leviticus, indeed, all of God's law. The Bible from beginning to end is filled with stories of God telling His people how to lead happy lives, helping His children get back on their feet when they fail. It is the story of His divine intervention – healing the sick, defeating the enemies of righteousness, and above all sending His Son to seek and save the lost. It is the story of a Father's infinite love for His children. The Bible is the story of God's holiness at work.

The words, "You shall be holy," are the connection of all that follows:

1. Consideration of the needy,
2. Prompt payment of wages for reasonable hours worked,

3. Equal justice for rich and poor,
4. Honorable dealings with our fellow man,
5. No malice or tale bearing,
6. Love of our neighbors,
7. Cordial dealings with strangers,
8. Just measures and balances in business.

Human life is an indivisible whole. From what we are to eat, to standards for cleanliness, to instructions for rituals, to principles of justice, God declines to exclude any of His people's activities from His law. While many people think God is just for the special times they need Him, the fact that God's law covers the simplest and most common detail demonstrates just how complete He expects our holiness to be.

Charity

Temporarily, I am going to skip over Leviticus 19:5-8 concerning sacrifice because I want to cover several New Testament passages before I visit this form of worship. We now move to verses 9-10 concerning charity or consideration of the poor.

> When you reap the harvest of your land, you shall not wholly reap the corners of your field, nor shall you gather the gleanings of your harvest. And you shall not glean your vineyard, nor shall you gather every grape of your vineyard; you shall leave them for the poor and the stranger: I am the LORD your God.

In these verses, we see that God was legislating charity and consideration for the poor at a time when all the other legal systems of the world were about safeguarding the rights of the wealthier classes. Introduced earlier in this chapter was the idea of human equality. This equality demands responsibility to each other.

We must help the poor. Poverty is dehumanizing. Poverty forces a person to focus his or her attention exclusively on fulfilling physical needs. Poverty has the effect of consuming so much of our effort that we have no time for those things that make us godly. Poverty can make us act like animals hunting for our next meal rather than men and women serving each other and serving God.

Unfortunately, sustenance sometimes is not a function of

4 : The Holiness Code

our merit. Poor people and strangers are our brothers and sisters. When they are in need, we are to give ungrudgingly – not only with an open hand but also with an open heart. We take this concept for granted today. Nevertheless, the concept of charity started in Leviticus. God commands a statutory charge on our harvest. This statute does not exclude the joy of private and voluntary assistance for those fortunate enough to be able to do so. We are required to leave a portion of the harvest in the field where the poor and the stranger do not have to beg for it. Indeed, the poor and the stranger still have to gather-up the gleanings and process the produce. Thus, we are not depriving our brothers and sisters of the dignity of work, the missing link in modern welfare programs.

There are few human sensations as rewarding as helping someone to climb out of poverty. There are few human sensations as confidence-building to a man or woman as climbing out of poverty. Helping one another is a part of God's plan for our moral maturity.

Laws, Not Suggestions

Leviticus 19:10 closes with, "I am the Lord your God," which occurs sixteen times in this chapter. Each time this divine seal occurs, it enacts the law – activates its authority. This statement reminds us that this is a law and not a suggestion.

God does not ask us to obey His law if we agree with Him. God legislates these things. His laws are not options to obey only when we understand and agree. God believes in discipline. God takes the stance that if we do something often enough, it becomes a habit, and we reap the benefits. We discover the joy of living the life He intends for us. It is like tithing; who in his or her right mind thinks that God needs their money? God could give the poor and the disadvantaged whatever they needed, but He would be depriving us of the joy He knows we will get when we play by His rules.

The next few verses of this chapter restate some of the second tablet of the Decalogue, our duties toward our fellowman. I sometimes think people of our day see these duties as a burden. Frankly, these commandments set us free from an internal struggle with selfishness. Obeying these laws helps keep us at peace with ourselves.

Exploitation

"You shall not steal, nor deal falsely, nor lie to one another" (Leviticus 19:11). When God gave life to humanity, He also gave us the earth and all that is on and in it. That means God gave us the right to possessions and the responsibilities that go with possessions. Based in large part on loving our neighbors as ourselves, Christianity requires that we treat other people as we would like others to treat us. Stealing and lying grow out of the notion of exploitation, as if people exist to provide an opportunity for abuse and manipulation. God's rules are clear. Hold your fellowman's property and information as dear to you as you hold your own.

It sometimes seems unfortunate that moral laws are not as measurable as physical laws. If a person violates the law of gravity, the response is immediate. Moral laws are as rigid as are physical laws, but they are more lenient in terms of reaction time. One spontaneous penalty for stealing and lying is not being trusted or believed. Unfortunately, many are the thieves and the liars who have discovered this too late. Obeying God's law prevents many psychic struggles.

Responsibility to Others

"You shall not cheat your neighbor, nor rob him. The wages of him who is hired shall not remain with you all night until morning" (Leviticus 19:13). This Scripture is clearly about an employer's obligation to his or her employees. Here we find the improper treatment of laborers equated with fraud and robbery. "Each day you shall give him his wages, and not let the sun go down on it, for he is poor and has set his heart on it; lest he cry out against you to the LORD, and it be sin to you" (Deuteronomy 24:15).

God is serious about our being responsible for one another. Employees often stand almost helpless in front of their employers. We are neighbors; one of the greatest duties in life is the welfare and happiness of others. Employers have a better than average opportunity to advance that welfare and happiness. Here the Bible is telling the employer how dependent the employee may be upon him. God will hold the employer responsible if he does not treat the employee the way he would want to be treated.

People with Special Needs

"You shall not curse the deaf, nor put a stumbling block before the blind, but shall fear your God: I am the LORD" (Leviticus 19:14). Literally, one who cannot hear cannot vindicate his or her own character. Harming or making sport of the blind is the epitome of human callousness and cruelty.

Furthermore, "deaf" and "blind" have a second meaning; these terms can refer to the inexperienced, uninformed, uneducated, and morally weak. We are not to take advantage of those who are helpless or people who may be in difficult circumstances. This verse also covers putting uninformed people into dangerous positions and ends with a stern warning against leading such people astray or provoking such people into making a mistake; "fear your God" for He is the ultimate avenger of the helpless.

We find that with power comes accountability. The strong is accountable for his actions over the weak: the employer over the employee, the educated over the unlettered, the experienced over the innocent, even the clever over the not-so-bright. The inoffensive use of all power and authority are the marks of a man or woman who follows God's law. The godly person approaches power and authority humbly. God holds those with power over others to high standards. With advantage comes responsibility. Now we shall see that there is to be absolutely no advantage given to the powerful other than responsibility.

Justice is Blind in the Courts of the Lord

"You shall do no injustice in judgment. You shall not be partial to the poor, nor honor the person of the mighty. In righteousness you shall judge your neighbor" (Leviticus 19:15). With all its sympathy for the poor and disadvantaged, the law fears that justice might be outraged in favor of the poor. Justice requires sympathy and compassion to be silent. There is to be neither prejudice in favor of the poor, nor dread of offending the powerful. Justice puts every human on a scale of merit that refuses to condemn by appearances.

Justice requires equal treatment of all people. To establish a proper balance between competing claims, we are to eliminate arbitrary distinctions between individuals. This is true not only in our courts but also in our daily lives. We are to treat people the same without regard to their station in life. God's law rejects the idea of different codes of morality for oneself and others. There is to be no difference in our treatment of the great and the humble, the ruler, and the ruled, even the religious and the non-religious.

Gossip

Further, justice requires a society where falsehood is controlled by each individual acting responsibly and controlling that most difficult to control gift, the tongue. "Thou shalt not go up and down as a talebearer among thy people; neither shalt thou stand idly by the blood of thy neighbor; I am the LORD" (Leviticus 19:16, *The Pentateuch,* American Version, Jewish Publication Society, 1917).[1] We are not to pedal scandal and malicious hearsay. We are certainly not to swap gossip for gossip no matter how juicy. The truth is that gossips are a pestilence to society. Injurious gossip may do as much harm as slanderous defamation. Destroying a person's reputation is equivalent to murder because in doing so you attack that which is most dear to a decent person.

We are not even to repeat a truth told with malice. My best understanding of this Scripture is that we are never to even say something negative about another person, even if it is true, unless the person to whom we are speaking vitally needs the information. Words cause actions, or, quoting a saying I once heard: "the mouth makes the first move." If we hear something that is malicious, we should let it die by not repeating it.

Helping Those in Distress

The second part of Leviticus 19:16, "neither stand idly by the

---

1 Although this translation will not be familiar to most readers, I have used it because it picks up an important nuance, as discussed in the text, which is more difficult to discern in most English translations.

blood of thy brother," is a rule we do not have in American law. This verse says that God requires that we help someone in distress. This makes perfect sense. However, if you see an injured person, American law does not require us to stop and assist. In fact, many states have had to pass "good Samaritan laws" to protect those who do stop to help. God's law requires that a godly person not stand idly by watching with indifference while another human being is in mortal danger. We are to assist the person in danger.

It is the same with our testimony. If we are in possession of information that would free an innocent person, we are to speak up and present the evidence. Created in God's image, we are all to help see justice rendered. God calls us to action to attack evil, to prevent violence and injustice, to act against wickedness and to help the innocent. Moral action is required when any human being needs help. It is that simple.

Vengeance Belongs to God

"You shall not hate your brother in your heart. You shall surely rebuke your neighbor, and not bear sin because of him. You shall not take vengeance, nor bear any grudge against the children of your people, but you shall love your neighbor as yourself: I am the LORD" (Leviticus 19:17-18). Most of the hate in this world is unjustified and groundless. We are not to do anything that harms our fellowman. We are not to hate people. We cannot hate someone in our heart without giving that hatred some form of outward manifestation. We are unable to carry out the rest of the law toward our fellowman if we hate anyone.

Not only is this true for the individual, it is true for groups. Racial rivalry, religious bigotry, many forms of nationalism, sexism, and so forth petrify into organized malice. Witness the Jews. Hatred of the Jews goes back to ancient times and has often manifested itself in wrongdoings ranging from segregation into the ghettos of Europe to the genocide of Hitler. We see this same hatred drummed-up against the Jews routinely by a number of Moslem countries and demagogic leaders even today.

There is more. When we hate someone or some group, that hatred has negative psychological and physiological effects on us.

Hatred is one of the most destructive of emotions. Indeed, every time we think about why we hate a person or a group, we relive whatever reason we think we have for that hatred. We become the victim of our own thoughts over and over again. That is why we are not to bear a grudge or seek vengeance. I mean, even if someone has harmed us in some way, every time we remember that harm or seek vengeance or bear a grudge, we become victims again. In our minds, we relive the pain. Our emotions do not allow us to differentiate between the real and the imagined. Only by removing the hatred, through forgiveness, do we release the pain and remove the ability of the person or group to keep hurting us again and again. Forgiveness means we no longer victimize ourselves.

This reliving of our victimhood is one reason why God forbids us to seek vengeance. We shall not repay evil with evil. We are to return good for evil (Matthew 5:43-48). Jesus says that in so doing maybe we will make an enemy into a friend. Only forgiveness removes our sin of hatred. I once read that if we should find an enemy and a friend in distress, we are first to help our enemy. This is to subdue any desire for vengeance. Then we are to help our friend.

The Golden Rule

Verse eighteen ends with what we call the "golden rule," which is often stated as "love thy neighbor as thyself." This is the law of life for the godly. This passage defines how we are to think, speak, and act towards others. God did not say do unto others as they do unto us. God said to "do unto others as you would have them do unto you." We can only control our own actions. Our work, as a creation of God in His image, is to change the world into the kind of place God intends it to be.

The next few verses (through 19:25) have to do with agricultural laws, laws outlawing certain pagan practices and laws regarding slavery. I will return to these subjects later on in this book. I will especially discuss slavery. For now, I will only say that Hebrew slavery had nothing in common with slavery as practiced by the Egyptians, Romans, or early Americans. The Israelites had no prisons. They were concerned with rehabilitation. Hebrew slavery was a highly regulated way to have people earn their way back into society as they worked for the person they had offended.

False Gods

"You shall not...practice divination or soothsaying" (Leviticus 19:26). Divination has to do with incantations. Soothsaying is fortune-telling, predictions, belief in luck and charms. Divination and soothsaying are putting one's faith in the illogical; putting one's faith in an action that cannot possibly help. Divination and soothsaying are superstition – a notion maintained despite evidence to the contrary.

We are further warned, "Give no regard to mediums and familiar spirits; do not seek after them, to be defiled by them: I am the LORD your God" (Leviticus 19:31). "Familiar spirits" were the dead. We are not to try to communicate with the dead. The painful power of incantations, charms, magic, demonology, and ancestor worship crushed ancient life. The ancients would try anything to influence the gods. This law frees the godly person from superstition.

It amazes me to realize the number of people who, in our age of science, wear lucky hats, read astrological charts and routinely dial 1-900-psychic. Divination, soothsaying, séances, and superstition have no real existence. They are a farce. They are idols. God wants us to worship Him, to study His word, to pray in Jesus name to Him. God does not want us to be tempted, even in the least, by any practice that just may lead us away from the narrow path He knows is best for us.

Honor Our Elderly

"You shall rise before the aged and show deference to the old..." (Leviticus 19:32). Honor the old. They have lived nearly a lifetime, something the rest of us have not yet done. We are to show respect for their years. Even where there is no formal education, the old generally have matured through the wisdom gained from experience.

We are to seek out the advice of our elders' experience. "Ask your father, and he will show you; Your elders, and they will tell you" (Deuteronomy 32:7). In today's society, where the knowledge in so many fields is growing exponentially, we too often view the wisdom of the old as out of date, out of touch. Further, we worship youth and vitality. We are inclined to see the elderly as deteriorating, weak, and helpless. I often marvel that we will listen to the advice of a harebrained actor or rock star and not seek out the advice of our own parents. The Bible views this attitude as self-destructive. The elderly have experience in dealing with the emotions and trials of life that no textbook can capture or computer program duplicate. The elderly have ties to the past that we need to understand. They rarely have a personal agenda that could hamper their advice. Their vanity does not bias their counsel. The opinions of the elderly not only provide us with the wisdom of a lifetime, the guidance of the elderly usually comes with no strings attached and no selfish motives.

Finally, as we have already seen, the laws of God oblige us to give just treatment to society's weakest members. If we fail in our duties to our elders, we are less likely to succeed in our relationships with fellow human beings. If we continue our societal drift from caring for those whose physical capabilities have diminished, what will be in store for us when we are old enough to be considered elderly? God requires us to do unto others as we would have done unto us.

How to Treat Strangers

> When a stranger resides with you in your land, you shall not wrong him. The stranger who resides with you shall be to you as one of your own citizens; you shall love him as yourself, for you were strangers in the land of Egypt... (Leviticus 19:33-34).

The last verse reminded the Israelites of how well their father Jacob was treated by an early Pharaoh and how cruelly they were later treated as slaves. Jews, more than any other people, understand being a stranger in a foreign land.

Stressed thirty-six times in the Scripture, our duty to strangers is on par with our duties to orphans and widows. In most ancient cultures the stranger had no rights. Many modern societies diminish rights of aliens. God tells us that we are to treat others as we want to be treated. We are to protect a stranger even though he or she is not a member of our family, our social group, or our community. The stranger is a human being. Our treatment of the stranger, the alien, helps us discover our humanity. It is in our treatment of the stranger that we truly find out if we live by the golden rule. Our treatment of the stranger is the greatest test of our allegiance to God's most basic code, "love thy neighbor as thyself."

Being Trustworthy

"You shall do no injustice in judgment, in measurement of length, weight, or volume. You shall have honest scales, honest weights, an honest ephah, and an honest hin..." (Leviticus 19:35-36). The ephah was a dry measure somewhat larger than a bushel. The hin was a liquid measure somewhat larger than a gallon. We are to hold our fellow human being's property as dear to us as we hold our own. This law has to do with secretly cheating, with fine print and with flowery advertisements that paint a product as something it is not. This law covers buying items stolen or obtained illegally.

In studying the Pentateuch we find the person who steals from another individual is in better shape than someone who steals from the public because he or she can more easily go to that person, repent, and ask forgiveness. However, the person who steals from the public will have a difficult time making good to the many. That means people who are in the business of running public charities or administering government programs are under an unusually heavy burden to do what is right. God's law holds that cheaters bear the moral responsibility for the evil that ensues from his or her irresponsible actions. The greater the number of people affected by an immoral action, the greater responsibility the sinner bears.

When a religious person cheats in his or her personal or business transactions, that person not only discredits himself or herself but also discredits God. Therefore, one who handles the business dealings of a church must be both honest and godly. That person, by his or her godly behavior may point someone to faith or conversely, by sinful behavior, turn someone from faith.

Observe God's laws

"Therefore you shall observe all My statutes and all My judgments, and perform them: I am the LORD" (Leviticus 19:37). The Pentateuch is about deeds and not creeds. The law stresses that if we can manage ourselves, all else will follow. The law stresses the preference we should give to the needs of others. The law is about life here on earth. Our role is to obey God's will here "as it is in heaven." We are to live in a way that hastens the recognition that we are to put God and His rules of governing the world first.

Since deed grows out of creed, we may not ignore creed. "For as [one] thinks in his heart, so is he" (Proverbs 23:7). Without any belief, the law topples. Without a belief in "I am the LORD," the rational principles for following the law are without a starting point.

The 19th chapter of Leviticus summarizes the idea of human equality, the idea of consideration of the needy, of equal justice for rich and poor, of honorable dealings and ethical business practices. In other words, it introduces the golden rule, the rule that Christ regarded as the second most important idea in the law.

5 : Jesus, Our Role Model

*For we did not follow cunningly devised fables
when we made known to you
the power and coming of our Lord Jesus Christ,
but were eyewitnesses of His majesty (1:16).*
— The Apostle Peter

Consciously or unconsciously, when we are growing up we select role models; we adopt their outlook on life. Many young people select stars like singer/actress Madonna or the rich heiress Paris Hilton, regardless of the moral implications. Young and famous people all have followings. However, as a parent, I must ask the question: do I want my daughters idolizing Madonna or Paris Hilton? Would I want my son to think of either of these two as a potential wife? As a parent I would much rather see my children select Florence Nightingale or George Washington as role models. However, if I could make the choice for them, Jesus would be their role model.

The Perfect Role Model

Keeping in mind that the primary reason Jesus came to earth was to be our Savior and Lord, He nevertheless is the perfect role model. Making Jesus our role model is what sanctification is all about. Jesus is like His Father, and Jesus asks us to be like Him. Listen,

> My Father has been working until now, and I have been working.... Most assuredly, I say to you, the Son can do nothing of Himself, but what He sees the Father do; for whatever He does, the Son also does in like manner. For the Father loves the Son, and shows Him all things that He Himself does; and He will show Him greater works than these, that you may marvel (John 5:17, 19-20).

If Jesus can only do what His Father does, what about us? Jesus answers, "I am the vine, you are the branches. He who abides in Me, and I in him, bears much fruit; for without Me you can do nothing" (John 15:5). With Jesus, we can do much, without Him nothing. Here Jesus is asking us to have a close relationship with Him identical to His relationship with His Father. How wonderful!

Too long many Christians have settled for being saved, for knowing that they will be with Christ on judgment day; but salvation should be only the beginning. Christ is asking us to join Him in His world-changing work. Modeling our lives after Christ in sanctification is so much more than justification in our initial salvation. It is accepting the quest for Christlikeness. It is joining God the Father and His Son in being always at His work. It is being a branch of Christ, it is bearing fruit, it is not only life changing, it is world changing.

I hear people ask, "What is God's will for my life?" That is the wrong question. If you want to join Christ in His work, if you truly want sanctification, the only question is "What is God's will?" Once we know what God is doing, then we know what we must do. The focus must be on God, not "my life."

The New Covenant – Higher Expectations

Jesus gives us much information about how to live a sanctified life:

5 : Jesus, Our Role Model

> Do not think that I came to destroy the Law or the Prophets. I did not come to destroy but to fulfill. For assuredly, I say to you, till heaven and earth pass away, one jot or one tittle will by no means pass from the law till all is fulfilled. Whoever therefore breaks one of the least of these commandments, and teaches men so, shall be called least in the kingdom of heaven; but whoever does and teaches them, he shall be called great in the kingdom of heaven (Matthew 5:17-19).

We can complete Jesus' thought with what Paul says in Hebrews:

> For this is the covenant that I will make with the house of Israel after those days, says the Lord: I will put My laws in their mind and write them on their hearts... (Hebrews 8:7-13; 10:16; cf. Jeremiah 31:31, 33).

Under the New Covenant, through regeneration we become receptive to God's laws in our hearts; and then, as we study them, they become imprinted in our minds as permanently as words carved in stone. There they should become habits of life ready to bless us with happiness, joy, and wellbeing in a thousand ways. Keeping the laws and commandments of God is not the cause of salvation but the result.

Our role model, Jesus, lived beyond the letter of God's law. He is the example, the One in whose heart, along with the Father and Holy Spirit, the law was born and written. Let us look at some examples Christ gave us, examples of how the law written on our heart should affect us.

Anger

Jesus said, "You have heard that it was said to those of old, 'You shall not murder, and whoever murders will be in danger of the judgment.' But I say to you that whoever is angry with his brother without a cause shall be in danger of the judgment" (Matthew 5:21-22). Here Christ teaches that the spirit of the law is the really important thing, for that defines the true condition of the heart.

It is so easy for religious persons to congratulate themselves for keeping the law, "Thou shalt not murder," but that is not enough. We must quench any propensity to violence.

Be humble.

Why?

Anger usually precedes violence. Anger without a cause dehumanizes us. Selfish anger is not the kind of passion that one "created in the image of God" should have.

In the interest of biblical exactitude, however, before proceeding further we should recognize that not all anger is sinful. Paul distinguishes for us that all anger need not be sinful: "Be ye angry, and sin not..." (Ephesians 4:26). That would, of course, be anger that had a just cause. Jesus was sometimes angry (Mark 3:5), and this we would call "righteous indignation," which motivated His action against the desecration of the Temple when He said "The zeal of thine house hath eaten me up" (Psalm 69:9; see John 2:14-17, Matthew 21:12-13; Mark 11:15-17; Luke 19:45-46). The Scripture speaks often of God's anger, for example, "God is angry with the wicked every day" (Psalm 7:11). Righteous anger is a powerful emotion God gives us to motivate us – though never in temper, malice, or self interest – to the balanced resolution of problems as Jesus did.

Having said that, by far the majority of anger references and commandments in Scripture concern sinful anger, and in that sense I will discuss it below.

Anger is one of our most dangerous passions. Anger clouds our judgment. Anger lets us speak and act out of turn only to regret it later. Over the years, I have noticed that I get angry more easily with my friends and my loved ones than with my enemies. That does not make sense. At one time or another, anger has caused most of us to make fools of ourselves. Christianity is a practical religion. The rules Jesus obeyed aim to help us live a happier, more productive life.

Throughout the Sermon on the Mount (Matthew 5-7), Jesus uses the word for love translated from the Greek word *agape*. *Agape* means we are to love even the unworthy. True love is not merited love. Christian love is not to be selective. Christians are to love all people simply because God created all in His image. Anger is the opposite of *agape*. Only in extreme or limited circumstances is anger an appropriate response, and then we are to control our passion and handle the problem in an ethical manner.

Christ in Matthew 5:21-22 is telling us that anger is akin to and as wrong as murder. Christ tells and shows us the kind of mindset – obeying the spirit of the law – that can prevent us from making sinful mistakes in anger. This is a part of writing the law on our hearts.

Our Word Is Enough

Another rule for living that Jesus gives us has to do with the Third Commandment:

> Again you have heard that it was said to those of old, "You shall not swear falsely, but shall perform your oaths to the Lord." But I say to you, do not swear at all (Matthew 5:33-34).

Due to the superstitious nature of people in the time of Christ, pagans made vows before their gods. The Jews of the time had fallen into this same trap. The Third Commandment says, "You shall not take the name of the LORD your God in vain, for the LORD will not hold him guiltless who takes His name in vain" (Deuteronomy 5:11). The Third Commandment forbids us to dishonor God by invoking His name to attest to what is untrue, or by joining His name to anything frivolous or insincere. God is holy and His name is holy. Christ is saying we have to guard against frivolously using the precious name of God. Our word is enough. If we have to strengthen our promise with a vow in the name of God, something is wrong.

The Third Commandment also teaches us about the holiness of God. It concerns the sacred nature of our relationship with Him. It involves our responsibilities to Him. Jesus is saying that people should not be tempted to use God's name to gain advantage. For example, we are not to say "I swear by the name of God that what I say is true." "But let your 'Yes' be 'Yes,' and your 'No,' 'No.' For whatever is more than these is from the evil one" (Matthew 5:37).

Using God's name for inappropriate things is taking God's name in vain. Unlike God, we do not always have the power to accomplish what we would like to, mean to, or should accomplish. Using God's name to verify something we are about to do is dangerous. Profaning God's name can elicit cynicism, distrust, or disgust for God. A Christian's word should be enough. This is a part of writing the law on our hearts.

Lust

Continuing in the Sermon on the Mount, Jesus said:

> You have heard that it was said to those of old, "You shall not commit adultery." But I say to you that whoever looks at a woman to lust for her has already committed adultery with her in his heart (Matthew 5:27-28).

In Matthew 19:3-11 Jesus explains further. He says that marriage is to endure for a lifetime. Christ said that divorce is only permissible in cases of adultery and then it is not a requirement. Marriage is such an exclusive relationship that even to look at another lustfully is a sin.

The problem, i.e., the need we have in regard to God's purpose for marriage, is how to continue love after the marriage so that we realize the love, companionship and the fulfillment that marriage offers. How do we emphasize the life-long devotion and affection necessary to make marriage the happy, divine institution God intended it to be? Christ says that we must control our lust. The first imperative is to avoid getting into situations where we might be tempted to think in an adulterous manner.

The first Scripture in the Bible concerning the sacrament of marriage is found in Genesis 2:18-25:

> And the LORD God said, "It is not good that man should be alone; I will make him a helper comparable to him...." And the LORD God caused a deep sleep to fall on Adam, and he slept; and He took one of his ribs, and closed up the flesh in its place. Then the rib which the LORD God had taken from man He made into a woman, and He brought her to the man. And Adam said: "This is now bone of my bones And flesh of my flesh; She shall be called Woman, Because she was taken out of Man." Therefore a man shall leave his father and mother and be joined to his wife, and they shall become one flesh. And they were both naked, the man and his wife, and were not ashamed.

Please note that the literal translation of the word "helper" is "to match." The woman was a match for the man. The key part of this passage is, "Therefore shall a man leave his father and his mother and shall cleave unto his wife, and they shall be one flesh." That is to say that the bond between these two people, a husband and a wife, is to be closer than that of a child to a parent. The

5 : Jesus, Our Role Model

relationship is to be so close that the husband and the wife act as one person. Husband and wife complete one another physically, socially, and spiritually as "one flesh." Only through marriage can human personality reach its highest potential.

Note that Genesis says that the man and the woman "were both naked, the man and his wife, and were not ashamed." Man and woman were naked before God in the Garden of Eden, and since there was no sin involved, there was no shame involved.

Similarly, they were naked before each other. Why? It shows that husbands and wives, in the divine institution of marriage, are doing the will of God in the procreation process that God Himself commanded (Genesis 1:28). The nudity here is symbolic of frankness, self-giving, and honesty – baring all unashamedly.

You see God's plan for marriage is to preserve, perpetuate, and sanctify that which God created in His image. One created in God's image should not look lustfully at his or her neighbor or our brothers and sisters in Christ. Again, with the correct attitude, we would not need the law, for "the law is not made for a righteous person, but for the lawless" (1 Timothy 1:9).

On the other hand, in John 8:1-11, we find the story of a woman caught in adultery. We see people ready to stone this woman to death. Jesus asked her accusers to do the stoning if they were without sin. All of the would-be punishers dropped their stones and walked away. Jesus wants us to love sinners. This is a part of writing the law on our hearts.

The Scriptures quoted in this chapter make it clear that Jesus in no way contradicts the law in the Pentateuch. Indeed, Christ is uncompromising. As Messiah, Jesus claims the right to supplement the law, to draw out its principles, and to disclaim the false deductions people have drawn from the law. "I am not come to destroy, but to fulfill." We too may fulfill the law because God has written it on our hearts.

The Testimony of Peter and John

Peter wrote, "For we did not follow cunningly devised fables when we made known to you the power and coming of our Lord Jesus Christ, but were eyewitnesses of His majesty" (2 Peter 1:16).

And John confirmed, "That which was from the beginning, which we have heard, which we have seen with our eyes, which we have looked upon, and our hands have handled, of the word of life... that which we have seen and heard declare we unto you" (1 John 1:1-3).

Here both these eyewitnesses confirm the same reality. The Apostle John proclaimed what a wonder Jesus is, our ultimate role model.

John was so highly thought of by Jesus, that even while nailed to the cross, Jesus asked John to care for His Mother, Mary. That makes this Scripture a powerful witness. John not only lived with Jesus for three years as an Apostle, he cared for Mary from the time of the crucifixion until her death. John therefore had not only access to his own memories of Jesus; he had access to those things that Mary would have told him. So here we have the witness of the man who arguably had more knowledge about Jesus than any other person who ever lived.

Furthermore, John was the one Apostle who lived long enough to have experienced and reflected as much as was necessary to sort through and draw marvelous conclusions about Jesus. "He who has seen me [Jesus] has seen the Father" (John 14:9).

Through Jesus, we humans can see the invisible God. "For God has sent the Son into the world...that the world might be saved through Him" (John 3:17). If He is the Savior of the world, we certainly must look to Him to be our example and role model in life.

Recognized by the World

Even the secular world recognizes that Jesus is special. John Stuart Mill, a brilliant philosopher, economist, and founder of a school of Utilitarianism, was also an unbeliever who wrote numerous attacks against Christianity, Christ, and the Scriptures. However, in his later life he wrote:

> Christ is still left a unique figure, not more unlike all his precursors than his followers, even those who had the direct benefit of his teaching. It is of no use to say that Christ as exhibited in the Gospels is not historical, and that we know not how much of what is admirable has

been superseded by traditions of his followers...who among his Disciples, or among their proselytes, was capable of inventing the sayings ascribed to Jesus, or of imagining the life and character of the Gospels? Certainly not the fishermen of Galilee; and certainly not Paul, whose character and idiosyncrasies were of a totally different sort; still less the early Christian writers....

Another example, H. L. Mencken, once the editor of *American Mercury* magazine, also spoke from the unbelievers' point of view. Mencken said:

The story of Jesus...is touching beyond compare. It is indeed the most lovely story ever devised. Beside this the best you will find in [the] sacred literature of Moslem, Brahman, Paris, or Buddhism seem flat, stale and unprofitable.

Our Great Commission

Christ, our role model, came and gave us the Great Commission, our mission:

All authority has been given to Me in heaven and on earth. Go therefore and make disciples of all the nations, baptizing them in the name of the Father and of the Son and of the Holy Spirit, and teaching them to observe all things that I have commanded you (Matthew 28:18-20).

Jesus spent His entire career preparing His Apostles and followers to go out into the world and spread God's message. Christ's very last words instructed His followers to convert the entire world. Christ called the Apostle Paul to go to the Gentiles, and Christ continues today to call missionaries to deliver His message "to the very ends of the earth." God wants all the men and women of the world to be saved and know the fullness of a sanctified life. God is Creator of all humanity. He wants what is best for His children and all people. Christ is His vehicle for salvation and the role model, bringing about the Garden of Eden on earth that God intended when He originally created the world.

I am emphasizing the Great Commission as a part of sanctification because so many Christians have lost sight of their obligation to spread the Good News. One example which proves that a Christian's primary work is spreading the Gospel is the obvious impact of the Great Commission on the apostles. After Pentecost, the apostles eventually went to the ends of the known world. The following list gives some of the missionary reaches which, according to tradition, were made by the apostles:

1. Simon Peter went to Rome.
2. Andrew went to Greece.
3. James, the son of Zebedee, went to Spain.
4. John went to Turkey.
5. Philip went to France.
6. Bartholomew and Thomas went to different parts of India.
7. Matthew went to Egypt.
8. James, Son of Alphaeus, went to Syria.
9. Jude/Thaddaeus went to Persia.
10. Simon, the Canaanite, went to Britain.
11. Matthias went to the Eastern Roman Empire.

All of the apostles honored the Great Commission. Other influential Christians also hit the missionary trail. John Mark went to Alexandria. Mary of Magdala went to Rome. Luke and Paul went to Greece and Turkey. Lazarus went to France and Britain.

The law was written on the hearts of each of these people. The message they spread is the universal faith. It is the faith that will let human kind live in peace, to reach the goals God wants His children to reach. What a wonderful role model we have in Jesus our Lord.

6 : The Pauline Epistles:
The Heart of New Testament Sanctification

The teachings of Christ far transcend
  all the teachings of the saints,
and who-so-ever has His spirit will discover,
  concealed in it, heavenly manna.
But many people, although they often hear the Gospel,
  feel little desire to follow it....
         —Thomas A'Kempis

Like many automobile drivers, I read bumper stickers. I particularly remember one; it read, "Christians are no different, just forgiven." Is that how it should be, no different, just forgiven? That seems so empty – to think that the only difference between the non-Christian and the Christian is that the Christian has accepted salvation. The people who feel this way need to investigate the treasures of God's grace; He forgives, He regenerates, He justifies. But now you need to understand and embrace the Holy Spirit's progressive work of sanctification in your life. In salvation we are instantaneously separated from the eternal penalty of our sins through justification by faith (Rom. 4:1-8), but then God commands us to begin a lifetime process of growth – personal sanctification, i.e., a progressive separation from the practice of sin. If you have not realized this, what joy and blessedness awaits you as God writes the beauty of His law (parts of which we have examined in the preceding chapters) in your mind and life.

Salvation is accepting Christ. Sanctification is living Christ. Salvation is a new birth. Sanctification is growing, maturing after birth. Salvation is a new beginning. Sanctification is a lifelong pursuit. Salvation is the gift of God's love to you. Sanctification is the enduring gratitude of your love to Him.

What They Don't Tell Us

Maybe because modern life is fast, convenient, easy, instantly gratifying, we miss the complete Christian message. We can get a hamburger and a milkshake in only a minute. Laundry can be ready in an hour. We can communicate with people on the other side of the planet with the click-of-a-mouse. It is no wonder that when some television preacher tells us that all we need to do is accept Christ and our life will instantly be different, better, happier, we believe that preacher. But what these preachers neglect to discuss are the bad habits we take down the isle as we bow and ask Christ into our life. Though saved and filled with the Holy Spirit, we carry with us a lifetime of debilitating habits that we are to "put off" as we grow in Christlikeness. The Pauline epistles tell us how we may join the Spirit in its further work of grace, the removing of our carnal conduct, as we become wholly the Lord's.

However, we need a few words of background. In Leviticus 19:2b we read, "Ye shall be holy: for I the Lord God am holy" . In Matthew 5:48 Christ repeated this, "Be ye therefore perfect, even as your Father which is in heaven is perfect." We read these calls for perfection, but we know we continue our bad habits after salvation.

Paul explains this lack of perfection after salvation. He says that even though saved, we are babes in Christ, immature.

> And I, brethren, could not speak to you as to spiritual people but as to carnal, as to babes in Christ. I fed you with milk and not with solid food; for until now you were not able to receive it, and even now you are still not able; for you are still carnal. For where there are envy, strife, and divisions among you, are you not carnal and behaving like mere men? For when one says, "I am of Paul," and another, "I am of Apollos," are you not carnal? (I Corinthians 3:1-4).

Yes, though saved, many remain carnal.

Not only are we carnal, we are imperfect (1 John 1:8, 10) in both faith and love.

> For what thanks can we render to God for you…night and day praying exceedingly that we may see your face and perfect what is lacking in your faith?…And may the Lord make you increase and abound in love to one another and to all, just as we do to you, so that He may establish your hearts blameless in holiness before our God (I Thessalonians 3:9-13a).

We see that though saved, we are still carnal, weak in faith and have not learned to love all people.

This exists in us because we are human, descendants of Adam. Though we are in Christ, we still carry Adam's nature until we die (1 Corinthians 15:22).

Nowhere is the carnal nature of man more apparent than in our society today. "Girls Gone Wild" is a popular example, on television and the internet. Pornography in all of its vile forms is so addictive that even some church members are snared. The examples are virtually innumerable.

Sanctification is All About Change

Paul says that Christians can change! We are commanded to *put off the old man* and *put on the new man.*

> If indeed you have heard Him and have been taught by Him, as the truth is in Jesus: that you *put off,* concerning your former conduct, *the old man* which grows corrupt according to the deceitful lusts, and be renewed in the spirit of your mind, and that you *put on the new man* which was created according to God, in true righteousness and holiness (Ephesians 4:21-24).

The old man reflects our ego, our natural self, our fleshly desires, and our corrupt adamic nature. The new man is Christlike, "which after God is created in righteousness and true holiness" (Eph. 4:24).

Paul repeats this same process to the Colossians in even stronger language (3:5-14). There he describes the character and nature of both the old man and the new man.

> Therefore put to death your members which are on the earth: fornication, uncleanness, passion, evil desire, and covetousness, which is idolatry. Because of these things the wrath of God is coming upon the sons of disobedience, in which you yourselves once walked when you lived in them. But now you yourselves are to put off all these: anger, wrath, malice, blasphemy, filthy language out of your mouth. Do not lie to one another, since you have put off the old man with his deeds...(Colossians 3:5-9).

Moreover, Paul gives the characteristics of the new man starting in verse 10 and culminating in verse 14 with the magnificent crescendo of the greatest commandment – love.

In verses 3:12-14, Paul describes the new man's character and nature:

> Therefore, as the elect of God, holy and beloved, put on tender mercies, kindness, humility, meekness, longsuffering; bearing with one another, and forgiving one another, if anyone has a complaint against another; even as Christ forgave you, so you also must do. But above all these things put on love, which is the bond of perfection.

God's will for humankind is Christlike perfection, perfection not of intellect, personality, or service, but full maturity (Gk. *telos*: completeness, maturity) of character, motive, and love of God and humanity.

What hope this gives to the young Christian struggling with innumerable temptations of the flesh. In so few words Paul takes us from the baser nature of the flesh to the apex of the nature of Christ – His *agape* love. It takes only minutes to read but years to master, yet the blessings begin as you, through the Spirit, resist your first sin.

Again, after finishing the great Roman chapters on justification by grace through faith (3-5), in typical Pauline fashion, he turned in chapter six to the principles of personal sanctification.

When Christ died for our sins, our old man judicially died with Him. Grace, not law, is the grounds for our salvation, and all this calls for a change in our behavior:

> Likewise you also, reckon yourselves to be dead indeed to sin, but alive to God in Christ Jesus our Lord. Therefore do not let sin reign in your mortal body, that you should obey it in its lusts. And do not present your members as instruments of unrighteousness to sin, but present yourselves to God as being alive from the dead, and your members as instruments of righteousness to God. For sin shall not have dominion over you, for you are not under law but under grace (Romans 6:11-14).

It is clear from this passage that salvation takes place as an instantaneous act rather than a process. Further, we are not to look to the old man for our motivation, but rather our motivation for righteous behavior is gratitude to God for our standing in grace. Furthermore, we must let the Bible, its study, and the Holy Spirit guide and help us to become in our external behavior the same as the new person God has created in our heart. This correlates with the principles of the New Covenant: God writes the love of His law in our hearts through regeneration; but through study of the Bible and the help of the Holy Spirit, His law is placed in our minds to guide our behavior.

Then again in Romans 12:1-2, Paul returns to matters of personal sanctification:

> I beseech you therefore, brethren, by the mercies of God, that ye present your bodies a living sacrifice, holy, acceptable to God, which is your reasonable service. And do not be conformed to this world, but be transformed by the renewing of your mind, that you may prove what is that good and acceptable and perfect will of God.

Christ purchased us on Calvary. We owe Him our all. We are to stop being servants of our own lusts and become His servants. When the Christian by faith offers himself or herself as a living sacrifice, the Holy Spirit cleanses the carnal nature and begins making us literally into a new person, empowering this new person for service. However, putting off the old man and putting on the new man is rarely easy.

Jay Adams and the "Hab" Twins, De and Re

Think about it this way: we are to replace every bad habit with a new good habit. A good little mnemonic device is to think of habits as twin brothers, De Hab and Re Hab. But poor De is bad, and we must not run with him. Re is good but very hard to get to know. We are to "put off" or dehabituate from sinful habits and "put on" or rehabituate in righteous habits as Paul has outlined for us. As we do this, we inch our way toward Christlikeness.

Dr. Jay E. Adams, in his book *The Christian Counselor's Manual*, extrapolates from the fourth chapter of Ephesians a clarification: When is a liar not a liar? When he or she is not lying? No. It is when that person becomes a *truth teller*. When is a thief not a thief? When he is not stealing? No. It is when he is *working* for his needs.

> Let him who stole steal no longer, but rather let him labor, working with his hands what is good, that he may have something to give him who has need (Ephesians 4:28).

Dr. Adams says God gave us the capacity to form habits. When we do something long enough it becomes automatic, a habit; we do not have to think about it, we just do it. That works great for things like driving a car. We can drive almost automatically while listening to the radio or carrying on a conversation. However, this capacity to form habits does not know the difference between the habit of being greedy or the habit of giving freely, between the habit of pride or the habit of humility.

We all have some sinful habits; we must replace them with positive, Christlike habits. For this reason the psalmist said: "Your word I have hidden in my heart, That I might not sin against You" (Psalm 119:11). When the Word is hidden in your heart the right action is spontaneous.

We must identify our sinful habits, Adams continues, as well as identify with what we will replace those sinful habits. Paul says this is the purpose of the law, to help us identify what is sinful. "What shall we say then? Is the law sin? Certainly not! On the contrary, I would not have known sin except through the law. For I would not have known covetousness unless the law had said, 'You shall not covet'" (Romans 7:7). Also we can know God's will; Paul wrote, "...do not be conformed to this world, but be transformed by the renewing of your mind, that you may prove what is that good and acceptable and perfect will of God" (Romans 12:2). In this way we are to use the law to distinguish our bad habits from the will of God, as exemplified by the life of Christ. This identifies the good habits that will replace the bad habits.

Dr. Adams notes that a part of growth in Christlikeness is to realize that we are captives of that which we know is wrong – captives of what we do not want for ourselves. Paul discusses this matter as a struggle within:

> ...For what I will to do, that I do not practice; but what I hate, that I do. If, then, I do what I will not to do, I agree with the law that it is good. But now, it is no longer I who do it, but sin that dwells in me (Romans 7:15-17).

Adams also points out that if we wish to be good athletes, we must start at the beginner's level, learn our sport, practice, and over the years advance. It is a long, disciplined journey filled with vicissitudes. So it is with sanctification.

> But reject profane and old wives' fables, and exercise yourself toward godliness. For bodily exercise profits a little, but godliness is profitable for all things, having promise of the life that now is and of that which is to come (I Timothy 4:7-8).

That is to say, breaking old habits is tough. It takes discipline, dedication, and time.

"Not by Might, Nor By Power..."

However, our effort can make it seem that sanctification is *our* work. This is a denial of the basic fact that both salvation and sanctification are by *faith*. To reduce sanctification to something we can accomplish without the help and guidance of the Holy Spirit is to put it into human hands where it will fail. The "do-it-myself" kind of thinking is fallacious: "But the just shall live by his faith" (Habakkuk 2:4). We must walk by faith; for "...without faith it is impossible to please him: for he that cometh to God must believe that he is, and that he is a rewarder of them that diligently seek him" (Hebrews 11:6).

The Holy Spirit, however, is the power behind sanctification:

> For this is the will of God, even your sanctification, that ye should abstain from fornication.... For God hath not called us to uncleanness, but unto holiness. He therefore that despiseth, despiseth not man, but God, who hath also given unto us his Holy Spirit (I Thessalonians 4:3, 7-8).

Holiness, however, is not an option; holiness is the will of God. It is the work of the Holy Spirit. The only condition for receiving the Holy Spirit is faith. The Holy Spirit will succeed in bringing us into conformity with Christlikeness. God wants us to join the Spirit in our sanctification because God wants us to be able to share the greatness of His work with others. "My Father has been working until now, and I have been working" (John 5:17).

All these things are so important – we have been doing those things that we now want to stop doing. The Holy Spirit works to replace those bad habits with good habits. God wants us to join the Holy Spirit in this sanctification so that we gain the delight and experience that participation brings as we join God in His work. That participation manifests itself in changes in our actions, attitudes and service. The experience allows us to understand and follow the whole purpose of God. We no longer have to please ourselves. We are now working with the Holy Spirit to please Almighty God. "For we are labourers together with God...." (1 Corinthians 3:9).

The Advent of the Paraclete

Although the Holy Spirit in His normative work of regeneration has been working with believers since the days of Adam, He came in His special role as Paraclete (comforter, helper, Gk. *parakletos*, see John 16:7) first at Pentecost.

> When the Day of Pentecost had fully come, they were all with one accord in one place. And suddenly there came a sound from heaven, as of a rushing mighty wind, and it filled the whole house where they were sitting. Then there appeared to them divided tongues, as of fire, and one sat upon each of them. And they were all filled with the Holy Spirit and began to speak with other tongues, as the Spirit gave them utterance (Acts 2:1-4).

Thomas Cook, in his classic *New Testament Holiness*, observes:

The visible tongues of fire were only emblems of what had passed within. What new creatures they then became! They met together as the sincere but timid and partially enlightened followers of Christ, but they left the upper room full of light, and power, and love. They were now filled with the Holy Ghost as all-illuminating, all-strengthening, all-sanctifying presence. The baptism of fire has consumed their inward depravity, subsidizing all their faculties, and filled to the full each capacity with divine energy and life.

John Wesley said, "The title 'holy,' applied to the Spirit of God, does not only denote that he is holy in his nature, but that he makes us so; that he is the great fountain of holiness to his Church." The Holy Spirit brings the power to live a holy life in an unholy world. The Spirit's work identifies us as a part with God's kingdom making us witnesses in our communities.

When the Holy Spirit filled the early Christians at Pentecost, they still had problems with bad habits. We see this in Acts where these people had trouble getting along; Peter and Paul had disagreements; and Paul had a thorn in the flesh. When John Wesley came along seventeen hundred years later, he felt his heart strangely warmed by the Holy Spirit and yet he had problems. If the filling of these people by the Holy Spirit did not suddenly perfect them, why is Pentecost one of the great days in human history? What about Wesley? What then did the Holy Spirit change about these people? Answer: Their witness exploded! The blast went around the world! On Pentecost, three thousand came to Christ with many immediately becoming missionaries, carrying their witness over the world. John Wesley's witness caused revival in England that changed the face of that nation. We may conclude from this that among the first works of sanctification is witness.

Ye Shall be Witnesses Unto Me

There are those who believe that God reveals Himself to the present generation through the Scriptures alone. This tends to make Christianity a cold, intellectual matter, divorced from real life. This is not Scriptural. Our witness is possible because the Spirit is in us.

Now we have received, not the spirit of the world, but the Spirit who is from God, that we might know the things that have been freely given to us by God. These things we also speak, not in words which man's wisdom teaches but which the Holy Spirit teaches, comparing spiritual things with spiritual (I Corinthians 2:12-13).

W. T. Purkiser in *Exploring Our Christian Faith* states:

> This witness is not an emotion, an exhilarator, an ecstasy of joy, although it may result in such feelings. It is not an outward manifestation or demonstration. It is an inward conviction that what God hath promised, that He hath performed, that the work of cleansing has been completed, and that the Holy Spirit abides in all the glories of His sanctifying lordship.

This conviction, this understanding, makes the witness of the Christian experiencing sanctification as natural and necessary as breathing.

When witnessing, keep in mind that people do not necessarily accept Christ the first, second, third, tenth, or seventieth time we witness to them. We do not know who else may have witnessed to them, who will witness to them, or how many times this has or will happen. It does not matter. Our job is to witness. So do not get discouraged. Some people may accept Christ at the first experience and others never at all. Our job is not to save people; we cannot save anyone. Only the Holy Spirit can do that. Our job is to join God in His work by witnessing.

Sanctification writes the Great Commission (Matthew 28:18-20) on our hearts in large letters. Jesus said, "...as my Father hath sent me, even so send I you" (John 20:21). "For we cannot but speak the things which we have seen and heard" (Acts 4:20). "But sanctify the Lord God in your hearts, and always be ready to give a defense to everyone who asks you a reason for the hope that is in you, with meekness and fear" (I Peter 3:15). See also Colossians 4:6; Romans 12:11; I Corinthians 9:19; on and on the Bible speaks of the naturalness of a Christian's witness.

However, like the bad habits spoken of earlier in this chapter, some of us have formed a bad habit: silence. With the help of the Holy Spirit, we may break this old habit of silence and replace it with our witness.

Think about it another way, had the disciples spoken up when Christ was in front of Pontius Pilate, Pilate might have freed Jesus. The silence of His witnesses may be the immediate reason the Romans hung Christ on the cross. "Therefore, to him who knows to do good and does not do it, to him it is sin" (James 4:17). Do not have the heavy burden of a lost soul on your conscience. Witness.

Fruit Unto Holiness

Beyond the joy of being ready to witness, what may the people experiencing sanctification expect? Will we be angelic? Or will we be unchanged? The Scriptures tell us that neither of these is correct. "But now having been set free from sin, and having become slaves of God, you have your fruit to holiness, and the end, everlasting life" (Romans 6:22). This passage seems to indicate that being "free from sin" may mean that our hearts lose the desire to sin – or at least that the desire to sin can be so greatly diminished as to have no power over you. There have long been differences of opinion among Christians concerning the possibility of reaching a state of "sinless perfection" in this life. And it seems that both human experience and Scripture answers in the negative. We remember Paul's comments in Philippians 3:12-14 (discussed below). But the Apostle John has pretty much settled the matter for most Christians when he said,

> If we say that we have no sin, we deceive ourselves, and the truth is not in us. If we confess our sins, He is faithful and just to forgive us our sins and to cleanse us from all unrighteousness. If we say that we have not sinned, we make Him a liar, and His word is not in us (1 John 1:8-10).

Yet, some people it seems want to use such a statement to dismiss the vast and voluminous teachings of Scripture on sanctification, but that is absolutely untenable theologically. Next to the work of Christ on the cross and the resultant doctrines of salvation by grace through faith, it seems self-evident that the doctrine of personal, progressive sanctification of the believer (though we never reach sinless perfection in this life) must be second in biblical emphasis right after salvation itself.

As indicated by the passage from Romans 6:22 (and many others) cited above, there is a high order of holiness to be experienced in this life. This, we believe, is indicated by another word (which has been ignored by many theologians) used several times in Scripture to express that high order of sanctification but not "sinless perfection." That is the word *blameless*. For example:

> And they [Elizabeth and Zacharias] were both righteous before God, walking in all the commandments and ordinances of the Lord *blameless*.

> That ye may be *blameless* and harmless, the sons of God, *without rebuke*, in the midst of a crooked and perverse nation, among whom ye shine as lights in the world (Philippians 2:15).

That word (see also 1 Timothy 3:2, 10; Titus 1:6) indicates a walk of righteousness so close to the Lord that a person with ordinary discernment would not be able to find a reason to blame such a person; he is "without rebuke." The word is sometimes translated *unimpeachable*.

Thus, we are not removed from the world nor are we wholly free from its temptations, but we can be free from the cruel whiplash and the ruthless dominion of sin. "For sin shall not have dominion over you..." It cannot rule you, but you can rule it.

Therefore, we are ready to be more of a man, more of a woman, than we could ever have been when our desires were not on the great things God wants us to do. Our old selves were selfish and centered on the things sinners find entertaining. Our new selves see the Garden of Eden God would have this world be. Our old selves lived in a world where each person had to look out for number one. Our new selves work for a different world. "Let no one seek his own, but each one the other's well-being" (I Corinthians 10:24). Thus we become true servants of God.

Gifts of the Spirit

As this growth moves forward, the Holy Spirit gives us gifts.

> For I say, through the grace given to me, to everyone who is among you, not to think of himself more highly than he ought to think, but to think soberly, as God has dealt to each one a measure of faith. For as we have many members in one body, but all the members do not have the same function, so we, being many, are one body in Christ,

and individually members of one another. Having then gifts differing according to the grace that is given to us, let us use them: if prophecy, let us prophesy in proportion to our faith; or ministry, let us use it in our ministering; he who teaches, in teaching; he who exhorts, in exhortation; he who gives, with liberality; he who leads, with diligence; he who shows mercy, with cheerfulness (Romans 12:3-8).

Note the sober judgment Paul asked us to have toward them. Note also that Paul places a high value on faith. Then Paul writes about the many gifts God gives. Except for the gift of prophesy, from the world's point of view, none of these gifts seems special or spiritual, but they are: serving, teaching, encouraging, giving to others, leadership, and showing mercy. These are the things Jesus did.

Many of those who watched Jesus' crucifixion wanted to see Jesus, while hanging from the cross by His nail torn flesh, perform a miracle. The world still wants entertainment, some sort of magic show, some sort of special power to prove we have the Holy Spirit. But God is about giving the world what it needs, not what it wants. The gifts the Holy Spirit gives us are exactly what the world needs.

The Fruit of the Spirit

Jesus did not take His disciples out of the world. He asked them to be the salt, the light of the world. He asked them to bear fruit:

> But the fruit of the Spirit is love, joy, peace, longsuffering, kindness, goodness, faithfulness, gentleness, self-control. Against such there is no law (Galatians 5:22-23).

The sanctified person is ready to suffer to help someone in need, to be gentle, good and faithful to that person's needs. We joy in helping others, in helping them find peace. We are meek, ready to perform the most humble task. We are ready to deny ourselves to help others. Instead of being self-centered, we seek to help others. Though in the world, sanctification makes us different from the world – different in motives, attitudes, habits, and relationships. Persons in need sense this; they experience Christ through us, His servants.

Treasure in Earthen Vessels

As we grow, ironically, we become more conscious of our human weaknesses. We can see the beauty of God's perfect holiness more clearly, and in the dazzling white light of Christ we do not show up as well as we once thought. This forces us to rely more and more on the power of the Holy Spirit.

Sanctification requires yielding any preferences we have for worldly things to God's will, humbling ourselves before Him and dedicating ourselves to being servants to His people, all of them, the saved and unsaved alike. So as servants, it behooves us to realize that at best we are earthen vessels.

Even the Apostle Paul, whom God used to write more of the New Testament than any other man, realized he had not yet "arrived." But still pressing on he said, "I press toward the mark for the prize of the high calling of God in Christ Jesus" (Philippians 3:14). Paul was blameless in the sense of having a clear heart, pure motives, and thorough devotion to the will of God. Nevertheless, he was not perfect in the sense of having reached the point where his course was completed or his attainments beyond improvement:

> Not that I have already attained, or am already perfected; but I press on, that I may lay hold of that for which Christ Jesus has also laid hold of me. Brethren, I do not count myself to have apprehended; but one thing I do, forgetting those things which are behind and reaching forward to those things which are ahead, I press toward the goal... (Philippians 3:12-13).

Paul knew that perfection and completeness of spiritual life was possible only in heaven, in the presence of the Savior. He knew glory awaited him when this earthen vessel had been laid aside. Meanwhile, he continued with Christ working here on earth; this work required him to continue to grow. God intends that we take Paul's approach. We will be God's partners! As His Holy Spirit guides us, we will do His work in this world.

Jesus prayed about this, and to this day we are the benefactors of this prayer:

> I have given them Your word; and the world has hated them because they are not of the world, just as I am not of the world. I do not pray

that You should take them out of the world, but that You should keep them from the evil one (John 17:14-15).

Jesus says that the world hated Him; so it will hate us. Simultaneously, Jesus asked God to protect us from worldly corruptions. As we grow to be more like Jesus, the world will treat us more like it treated Him. It goes with the territory.

Paul says something similar.

> But we have this treasure in earthen vessels, that the excellence of the power may be of God and not of us. We are hard-pressed on every side, yet not crushed; we are perplexed, but not in despair; persecuted, but not forsaken; struck down, but not destroyed – always carrying about in the body the dying of the Lord Jesus, that the life of Jesus also may be manifested in our body (II Corinthians 4:7-10).

Paul, like Jesus, warned of difficult times. Paul also speaks of the church as Christ's body.

Both Jesus and Paul knew, though it seems incredible, that God will use us to change the world.

> Most assuredly, I say to you, he who believes in Me, the works that I do he will do also; and greater works than these he will do, because I go to My Father. And whatever you ask in My name, that I will do, that the Father may be glorified in the Son (John 14:12-13).

Look at the world. Is this the heritage we want to leave our children? The world needs revival. God, through His Holy Spirit, gives us the opportunity to join this great work. Christians you must stop letting the world fill you; instead, you fill the world!

Let the Holy Spirit continue His further work of grace in you, equipping you to be an effective part of the Body of Christ. Yes, the world will hate us because it defends many of the sins that our love and witness of Christ will extinguish. Yes, we will be hard-pressed, but God wins.

So stop being satisfied with salvation alone; but with profound gratitude, get on your knees and tell the Holy Spirit that you are ready to grow, to serve, to sacrifice, and to win. Sanctification, while the most wonderful journey anyone can possibly undertake, is also the most difficult. But Jesus said, "If anyone desires to come after Me, let him deny himself, and take up his cross, and follow Me" (Matthew 16:24).

Pick-up your cross and go into a world that desperately needs an about face, a new direction, a revival of Godly proportions – and victory is certain.

7 : Prayer

But we saw, God, how men prayed to You and,
*   with our limited capacities,*
* we formed an impression of You as someone great,*
Who was able, even when not present to our senses,
*   to hear us and to help us.*
— The Confessions of Saint Augustine

If the modern world seems to interfere with your understanding of prayer, do not despair. Even though pagan Rome's multiple gods, superstitions, and magic dominated much of Augustine's world, Augustine learned to pray. Jesus' Apostles had a similar problem. "Now it came to pass, as He was praying in a certain place, when He ceased, that one of His disciples said to Him, 'Lord, teach us to pray, as John also taught his disciples'" (Luke 11:1). Jesus taught them that they might teach us.

Prayer begins early in religious homes. Children, as soon as they can speak, ask the blessings at meals and say their prayers before they go to sleep. "Now I lay me down to sleep; I pray the Lord my soul to keep. If I die before I wake, I pray the Lord my soul to take." Teaching prayer to children is as it should be; however, many people never advance beyond the childhood phase of prayer. This may lead to the idea that we can pray for anything and receive it. It is like the childhood prayer where a boy asks for an A on his report card or a girl asks for a Barbie doll. When we do not get these things, we say God said no to our prayer. Maybe God did not say no as much as we simply have not advanced in our understanding of prayer. If Augustine and the Apostles had to learn, there is no shame in admitting we too must learn.

Prayer is Not Magic

To begin, we must distinguish prayer from the "magic" of witchcraft or from asking the Roman gods for favors. Magic, so called, is about our will, not God's will. Magic is about the occult, using formulas, charms, and incantations to influence the gods, asking for material results. Magic invites false hopes and false means to achieve those hopes. The Bible clearly tells us that there is no such thing as magic. God is real; magic is not.

Yet, many treat prayer as if it is magic, as if anything they pray for will happen. This false attitude toward prayer is natural in a world dominated by the baser passions. We shun discipline and want to do our own thing. Material wants dominate our lives. Is it any wonder then that in most prayers people are asking for some sort of creature comfort?

Think about it. People do not hesitate to go to God and ask Him for some convenience, some tangible thing. People pray for everything from finding a close parking place at the local mall to winning the lottery. Unfortunately, this "give-me-what-I-want" kind of prayer is the single religious activity of many present-day Christians. This is wrong. This is what the Greeks and Romans expected from their gods. Prayer must be about glorifying God and not about our selfish desires.

Many people who pray regularly do not attempt to serve the Father, are not interested in Christian works, want nothing too exotic, and dislike the idea of change. These people do not expect or want sermons or churches that require that they examine their lives, give up some habits, or behave differently. The "good" god these people worship has more in common with the Greek god Zeus than with the God to whom Jesus taught us to pray.

God is not the more sophisticated, apathetic, emotionless, self-sufficient god of the philosophers. Christ warned us about a similar form of blasphemy: "And when you pray, you shall not be like the hypocrites. For they love to pray standing in the synagogues and on the corners of the streets, that they may be seen by men. Assuredly, I say to you, they have their reward" (Matthew 6:5).

Prayer Gets Objective Results

God is the Maker of the universe, yet He is concerned with the fate of widows and orphans. He knows even the sparrows. God cares passionately about what transpires on earth. That is why He reveals His will, enters into covenants, sends prophets, and constantly intercedes in the drama of history to get people to do His will. Prayer is about understanding what God is doing. He wants us to join Him, to do His will.

When we pray, we must remember, "'...My thoughts are not your thoughts, Nor are your ways My ways,' says the LORD" (Isaiah 55:8). Requests we think are small may be very important. You never know when the simplest act will bring someone to Christ or help someone in distress. Yet, the Lord has the power to handle huge matters beyond our ability to comprehend or imagine.

Daniel prayed for, and was granted, great understanding (9:1-27). Nehemiah prayed for, and was granted, the rebuilding of a nation (1:1-11). Elijah prayed for, and was granted, a miracle that defeated the prophets of Baal and a nation returned to God (I Kings 18:36-38). Hezekiah prayed for, and was granted, victory over Assyria (II Kings 19:14-38). Peter and John prayed for and were granted boldness in speech in spite of persecution (Acts 4:24-31). Paul prayed, and it was granted, that the people of Ephesus would know God in greater wisdom, knowledge, and enlightenment (Ephesians 1:16-23). There are examples of many answered prayers in the Bible. What do these prayers have in common that made them work for the glory of God?

There are, at least, four fundamental principles of prayer.

First. We must have faith that what we ask for we will be given: "Most assuredly, I say to you, he who believes in Me, the works that I do he will do also; and greater works than these he will do, because I go to My Father" (John 14:12).

Second. Notice in addition to having faith, Jesus says we must continue doing "the works" He was doing. We must be asking to do God's will, continuing His work.

Think about what the Bible states in its first verses (Genesis 1:1); God created all things. All things are for His purpose (Rev. 4:11). Christ was vitally involved in controlling God's creative process:

> In the beginning was the Word, and the Word was with God, and the Word was God. He was in the beginning with God. All things were made through Him, and without Him nothing was made that was made (John 1:1-3).

Christ was with God in the beginning. He is still with God, but now He is also our representative.

> Now this is the confidence that we have in Him, that if we ask anything according to His will, He hears us. And if we know that He hears us, whatever we ask, we know that we have the petitions that we have asked of Him (I John 5:14-15).

Third. We must ask in Christ's name. "And whatever you ask in My name, that I will do, that the Father may be glorified in the Son. If you ask anything in My name, I will do it" (John 14:13-14). Therefore, we must have faith, we must be doing or attempting to do God's will, we cannot only expect results, we are to expect results of divine proportions.

Prayer, then, is about objective results. It is about continuing Christ's work. It is not about subjective results or feel good results. However, we will feel good about a matter we pray about knowing that God's power and willingness will accomplish it. However, feeling good is not the objective – continuing Christ's work is the objective.

Fourth. Our prayers are in no way to reflect our own selfish desires, our sinfulness. God will not listen to such prayers.

> Behold, the LORD's hand is not shortened, That it cannot save; Nor His ear heavy, That it cannot hear. But your iniquities have separated

you from your God; And your sins have hidden His face from you, So that He will not hear (Isaiah 59:1-2).

If I regard iniquity in my heart, the Lord will not hear" (Psalms 66:18).

The Practical Side of Prayer

Now that we have covered four of the basics of prayer, we need to look at the practical side of prayer. Seeking God's will through prayer is both a gift and a task. Prayer is both struggling with God in the darkness and resting in the stillness – witness Jacob before his reunion with Esau. There is a time to plead – witness Abraham before the destruction of Sodom and Gomorrah. There is a time to beg, and there is a time to submit – witness Christ the night before His crucifixion.

Prayer can be a passionate pleading with God, even wrestling with God. God wants us to be covenant partners, not automatons. In this sense, prayer may seem to change the will of God. More fundamentally, prayer is an examining of our needs and desires so that we might be more fully conformed to His ultimate will and purpose.

We want our needs and desires to conform to His will. We want to set our goals to be in tune with His plan. Prayer is seeking a partnership with God. This is where many Christians misunderstand prayer. We are not praying for our desires. We are praying to know His desires, to put our desires in tune with His. Prayer is seeking God's will, seeking to know our part in His beautiful scheme of things.

Another practical issue in prayer is does God hear my prayer? Does my prayer move God? Does He answer prayer? Does He respond? Does He intervene? Often, a better set of questions is: Do I hear my prayer? Does my prayer move me? Am I trying to answer this prayer? Am I working to accomplish this prayer? Am I seeking what I can to accomplish this prayer?

If our prayer is so unimportant to us that we do not seek to join God in His work, we should not expect a favorable response. Unless we are helpless, we are to become engaged in God's work. Otherwise, we deny Him our God-given talents. To pray for things for which we are unwilling to work, is to attempt to turn God into a slave.

God blesses us with talents. Prayer is about achieving the potential of those talents. God also blessed us with weaknesses. Prayer is about achieving control over those weaknesses. Prayer shows God that we care about Him; we want to be His partner in continuing His objectives.

If we pray for someone who is hungry, we must be willing to help feed that person (James 2:15-16). Christ would. If we pray for the strength to get through one more day at a job we hate, then we must be willing to try to improve the job while we search for another. If we pray for knowledge and understanding, then we must be willing to study and think. These are the acts of someone who is joining God in His work.

In Hebrew, *avodah* is the term often used for prayer. *Avodah* means work. Prayer is about working to become the kind of person a child of God should be. Jesus said, "...ask, and it will be given to you: seek, and you will find; knock, and it will be opened to you" (Luke 11:9). That does not sound totally effortless.

Partners in Covenant

Prayer derives from the basic biblical affirmation of the divine image implanted in the human being: "So God created man in His own image...male and female He created them." Further, God put us in charge of His Garden of Eden "to tend and keep it." This root idea forms the common ground of discourse between the two significant partners in this covenant. The worshiper is not a blind thoughtless android, an ear into which God shouts orders. God created each of us with a purpose. Prayer is a way of discovering who we are and what our purpose is.

Prayer is a form of self-examination or self-judgment, concerned with correcting one's self or putting one's self in line with God's will. Our thoughts and actions are the targets of our prayers. Patience, discipline, self-control are proper goals of prayer. We may pray for Christlike thinking and behavior as means to achieve desired goals.

Think about it another way. The only one any of us can control is himself or herself. Most of us rarely do a good job at that. Yet God asked each of us sinners to be partners in His creation. When we pray for God's help, we are asking for a miracle. That is heavy – for mere sinners, earthlings, asking God Almighty, Ruler of the Universe, to do something especially for us. Out of the billions of people on earth, a tiny speck in the vastness of God's creation, we ask God to take time out to intervene on behalf of our request. Do we have the right to be so audacious? No, we do not have the right. Rather, we have an obligation because God, our Father, told us to do so. He wants us to pray to be Christlike.

The New Testament repeatedly tells us that Christ spent a great deal of time in prayer. He prayed, even when the answer meant He would suffer, to know God's will and to have the strength to do it. Whether our need is small or large, because God is God, and because we are human, it is probably good advice to think about what we are asking, to choose the miracles we ask for carefully and out of need for divine help rather than to pray frivolously. Most of us need this kind of help many times a day.

This is a sinful world. Evil has a strong, destructive hold on humanity. If a miracle is what we need to help break sin's hold, to return this world to the Garden of Eden God intends it to be, then nothing short of God-like success is worthy of prayer. "Yet you do not have because you do not ask" (James 4:2). As devout persons, we have an obligation to make as great an impact as is divinely possible. "With God, all things are possible."

Boldness in Prayer

When we are bold enough to go to God Almighty for a miracle, we must ask Him not only for guidance but also for guidance to be powerfully victorious. Prayer is not a time to be bashful. When we ask the Almighty for help in sharing His work on earth, let us not waste His time on a trivial response. We are not praying a selfish prayer. People of faith think differently than do others. It is not selfish to pray boldly. We are not praying for something that is self-centered. We are praying that God guide us sinners. This is not a time to hold back. We are not asking God for a Cadillac or to win at the slots in Las Vegas. We are asking God to help us be a part of what our Father wants His children to be, to do, to further His creation. We are not praying that God do all the work. We are praying for God to show us what He is doing so that we may join Him. We are praying to be successful for God. Our Father deserves the best we have. We want nothing more and nothing less than what God wants.

Be bold in prayer. A Christian worth his or her salt asks God to show him or her how to be wildly successful.

This kind of bold prayer works: "The hand of the Lord was with them, and a great number believed and turned to the Lord" (Acts 11:21; see also Joshua 4:24, Isaiah 59:1). Boldness in partnership with the Lord is not a vice. It is the mark of a true believer – "...he preached boldly..." (Acts 9:27; see also 4:13; 5:29; and 7:51). Only such boldness could have overtaken the decadence that was Rome.

Rome was not only a pagan society; it was a society built totally on selfishness. The Roman economy was powered by the labor of slaves captured by the Roman army. Its treasure houses were filled with the spoils of conquered lands. Its evenings were crammed with sexual perversion. Men slaughtering men and animals devouring children dominated its sports. The early Christians, often slaves themselves, overcame the power of Rome with the love of Christ because they were unashamed of praying boldly. So should we.

The Ultimate Example

In the balance of this chapter we examine our best example of prayer, the Lord's Prayer. Jesus constructed it with great care. Perhaps He foresaw that sincere people would erect walls of faulty doctrine between them and God; that people would attempt to dilute His simple teachings with theological devices. Jesus designed His prayer so that well-intentioned theologians could not weaken it. Jesus designed it to pass safely through the ages preserving the complete Christian message. Thus, through all the upheavals and disputes in Christian history, this prayer comes through uncorrupted, unspoiled, and full of meaning.

Jesus designed His prayer so that those who use it regularly will experience spiritual growth, the only growth that really matters. Further, this prayer meets everyone's need at his or her level. It provides rapid religious development for Christians sufficiently advanced to be ready for meat. In its surface meaning it supplies less spiritually minded people with just what they need the moment they are beginning to pray. The only people who do not profit from the Lord's Prayer are those who rattle it off like parrots.

> After this manner therefore pray ye: Our Father which art in heaven, Hallowed be thy name. Thy kingdom come. Thy will be done in earth, as it is in heaven. Give us this day our daily bread. And forgive us our debts, as we forgive our debtors. And lead us not into temptation, but deliver us from evil: For thine is the kingdom, and the power, and the glory, for ever. Amen (Matthew 6:9-13).

Our Father. The prayer begins with, "Our Father." "Our," a plural possessive pronoun, forces us to see the kinship of all believers. It forces our attention to the idea that all believers are the descendents of one Father. Moreover, in Christ, "There is neither Jew nor Greek, there is neither slave nor free, there is neither male nor female; for you are all one in Christ" (Gal. 3:28) – because all believers are brethren.

With "Our Father," Jesus is definitely describing the relationship of a parent and child. God is not a despot. We are not His slaves. He is "Our Father." We are His children. Jesus said,

> If you then, being evil, know how to give good gifts to your children, how much more will your Father who is in heaven give good things to those who ask Him! (Matthew 7:11; see also Luke 11:13).

Therefore, Christ begins His prayer by establishing the character of God as that of the perfect Father lovingly dealing with His children. Furthermore, "If God is for you, who can be against you." Since God is "Our Father," we need not fear anything.

This parent-child relationship forces us to remember that we should act as God would expect His children to act. We must realize that God made all people in His image. We should be ladies and gentlemen: polite, considerate, loving in everything we do. We should be as loving brothers and sisters to every human being on this earth.

In Heaven. "Our Father, which art in heaven," establishes the fundamental fact of God's existence. It is God's nature to be in the perfect place, heaven. It is the fundamental nature of humankind to be on the earth. God is cause and humankind is manifestation. It is humankind's destiny to express God in glorious ways. God originally put us in the Garden of Eden. His directions in the Garden of Eden were to work it and take care of it. Those are still His directions for earth for those who live in harmony with His purpose.

Hallowed. Then comes praise: "Hallowed be thy name." Hallowed means holy, or reverenced. In the Old Testament, a person's name indicated something of his or her character. God's name was absolutely holy. People spoke it only on the most special of occasions. This part of the prayer concerns how we are to take God's holy name upon our lips. In this part of the prayer we are taught the proper attitude in view of the fact that God is worthy of reverence – complete, perfect, altogether good.

Thy Kingdom Come. Our work in prayer is to express in concrete form the abstract ideas that God has furnished us in this model. He gave us creative power that we might join Him in His work. "Thy kingdom come" means that it is our duty to help establish God's kingdom on earth. The saying that, "God has a plan for everyone, and He has one for you" is quite correct. God has planned a splendid career, an interesting and joyful life for each of us. If we are not experiencing that fullness, we are likely out of sync with God's will. Moreover, the early mention of the Kingdom in the prayer, when considered in the light of Matthew 6:33, speaks also to our priorities in life.

Thy Will be Done. We see in our daily lives that people too often choose to use their free will to operate outside God's law, His guidelines. People allow themselves to think wrongly, selfishly. This approach eventually brings unhappiness. We must understand that it is our job to do His will, to be about His work. Our business is to bring our total nature into conformity with the will of God.

In Earth as it is in Heaven. Men and women should have the desire to fulfill the divine purpose on earth just as the divine purpose is fulfilled in heaven. The two, earth and heaven, are to be ruled as one. This rule, or dominion, of earth was commanded from the beginning (Genesis 1:26-28). We were to be God's vicegerents to rule His earth in righteousness and for His glory. That commandment has never changed, so naturally it is to be a continual object of work and prayer. It is God's will to walk again with redeemed humankind as He walked with Adam and Eve (Revelation 21:3). God wants earth to be as wonderful as heaven.

Give us this Day our Daily Bread. We live in continuous dependence on God for the food we must have for our existence. We cannot get bread once and then forget God. The symbolic meaning of "daily bread" is the realization that we need God's presence in our lives daily also. Just as faith "is the substance of things hoped for, the evidence of things not seen," God is the substance and sustenance behind our faith. He is the "manna." Regular prayer feeds our mind just as regular meals feed our bodies.

Another reason the bread symbol is such a telling one is the act of eating food is something we must do for ourselves. No one can assimilate food for us. Putting God into our life is a thing that no one else can do for us. The decision to accept God into our lives is ours alone. Then the Holy Spirit takes over.

And Forgive Us Our Debts, As We Forgive Our Debtors. Some translations say "And forgive us our sins, as we forgive those who have sinned against us." The use of the words "sins" and "debts" as synonyms is interesting. When we sin against God, do we owe Him a debt? Obviously, that is what asking for forgiveness is about, getting a debt removed. It is good that God's grace is complete, that He does forgive us completely. The Bible tells us that when God forgives us He removes even the memory of the sin.

Notice the word "as" in "forgive us our debts, as we forgive...." God says we are to do as He does, forgive and forget the sins of others against us. This thought is central to this prayer. Indeed, this thought is central to the teachings of Jesus Christ as He preached forgiveness. Christ here is saying, "Now, if you do not forgive from your heart, how can you expect God to forgive you?" Does this mean that God bases forgiveness on our own good works? No, but it does mean that if we are unwilling to forgive others, we are in no condition to ask God's forgiveness for ourselves.

Forviveness was the purpose of Christ's death. Our Lord went to the cross so God could justly forgive sinners. That is the message of the Gospel. We do not have to go around with the burden of anger and revenge interfering with our life. We do not have to carry guilt around.

We will have no trouble forgiving others if we are right in our relationship with our Father. Jesus leaves no room for doubt about this fundamental truth. As we set others free, we set ourselves free. Resentment is really a form of attachment. The cosmic truth is that it takes two to make sin work. Those who do not forgive others tear down the bridge on which they themselves will have to walk.

Deliver us from Evil. The next passage in the Lord's Prayer is: "And lead us not into temptation but deliver us from evil." This does not imply that God does sometimes tempt us. The books of James and Job assure us that God never tempts anyone. Rather, Jesus is encouraging an attitude that flees from temptation. The Christian recognizes his or her particular weakness and stays clear of situations that tempt his or her weakness.

I will remember as long as I live what one of the finest Christian ministers I ever knew told me one day when we were discussing temptation. I asked him if he was ever tempted and by what. Much to my astonishment, he said yes. He said he could not help but make a pass at a good-looking woman. I asked what he did. He said he avoided all women but his wife and children. In his church work, he took his wife with him on all visits to his female congregation members. He prayed daily that God would help him recognize quickly and flee immediately any situation where he might be able to act on his temptations. That is exactly the concern addressed in this part of the prayer. Just as an alcoholic must ask God for help every single day for the rest of his or her life to avoid alcohol, so each of us has some sin or sins we must avoid.

Jesus knew from His own personal experience in the wilderness about the power of temptation. The further we advance as Christians the greater the temptations that await us. Temptations such as pride, personal glory, material gains, personal preferences versus God's will are all situations that have tripped up many a fine Christian.

For Thine is the Kingdom. Finally, we have, "For thine is the kingdom, and the power, and the glory, forever." This last line sums up the omnipresence and the "allness" of God. It means God is the doer. He is the only real power. God is all. The sentence is a celebration, a turning to the light that is God. God was, is, and will be.

Prayer assures us that God's will is ultimate and unchanging. Prayer assures us that He wants us to be His partners. We are His children. He wants us to inherit all the splendor the world could be if humankind would pray and conform to God's will. Prayer is about asking God to help us conform to His plan.

8 : Major Contemporary Issues

If you'll just do like you are supposed to do,
you'll be much happier.
— My Mother, Martha Warren Houston, 1918-1982

Paul gives us an idea of how difficult the wonderful challenge of sanctification is, "...but I press on, that I may lay hold of that for which Christ Jesus has also laid hold of me. Brethren, I do not count myself to have apprehended..." (Philippians 3:12, 13). If Paul who by the time he wrote this passage has not reached his goal, how long will it take the rest of us?

We often forget that the only requirement to attend church is to be a sinner. All people are welcomed. Murderers are welcomed, drug addicts, drunks, adulterers, no sin is too great. Discrimination against a particular class of sinner is among the most horrible crimes a church can commit. Christ wants all sinners to come.

The only requirements for salvation are to confess our sins and to trust in Jesus as Savior and Lord of our life. Salvation makes us right with God, but it is just the beginning of the trip. Many of our sinful habits remain. After salvation, each of us must examine all facets of our life, searching for those remaining sinful habits, and then root them out one by one.

Furthermore, though saved out of a life of sin, we do not know how to identify our own sins. It is a false assertion that the sense of man is the measure of all things. Paul tells us that is what the law is for, that we might know what sin is. Once we have identified our own sins, sanctification then has targets for change.

Nowhere will the saved sinner moving toward sanctification find more targets, i.e., habits he or she needs to change, than in our contemporary world. Contemporary issues present many of us with challenges. Some of these issues are the subject of this chapter. As you read, see if you have any of these habits. Do you need to change?

Adultery

We start our examination with a prevalent sin, adultery. Adultery is any sex out of wedlock. The law against adultery clearly applies to single as well as married people. Adultery is not only any sex out of wedlock during marriage but also before marriage. Why? What is the harm in enjoying a little intimate relationship while courting? What is the harm? If no one finds out, what is wrong with a little affair while married?

The Joy of Waiting. I will begin my answer by relating a marriage of two Orthodox Jews I read about, a Rabbi and his wife. The Rabbi said that, while at times he and his wife found it difficult, they remained celibate until they were married. While both had dated a number of people, neither fooled around before they were engaged. After their engagement, while it was sometimes tempting not to, they continued to remain celibate until married.

They were in their early twenties when they wed and both, according to the Rabbi, were passionate beyond belief. Suddenly released were years of successfully controlling life's most powerful drive. He said they attempted to fulfill God's law to be fruitful and multiply at least once a day and, on the Sabbath, more often. They had fulfilled the seventh commandment.

They each saw the other not only as a friend but also as extremely sexually desirable. The Rabbi said he realized that because they had followed God's law before marriage, neither he nor his wife would ever be tempted to break this law after their marriage. He said he and his wife, when thinking of sexual relations, only thought of each other. There was no other memory in their minds – no idea that anyone else could fulfill his or her sexual needs and desires. They had learned to be passionate only for each other.

The Grief of Unbridled Lust. Contrast the story of the Rabbi and his wife with the story of another American couple. While growing up, the wife had a few "discreet" flings. The husband did also. Once they started dating each other, but before they got married, they routinely had sex, just with each other of course.

From day one of their marriage they had memories. They had learned that there were people other than their spouse with whom they could find some sort of sexual satisfaction. The Rabbi and his wife had no such memories.

Neither the husband nor the wife had learned to control their sexual desires when it was difficult. The Rabbi and his wife were masters over their passions. Once married the all-American husband, like many good husbands getting started, worked long hours and usually came home tired. He was not the companion his wife was expecting, not what he had been during their courtship. While the Rabbi's wife would have toughed this out, this wife had not developed that kind of discipline.

At a party one night she found a friend's husband, a co-worker of her husband, who made inappropriate sexual advances, and they began what she believed to be a discreet affair. She felt safe fooling around with a friend's mate. This minimized the likelihood of the affair being discovered. Now, since she was getting some sexual satisfaction outside her marriage, she was no longer passionate toward her husband.

This was clearly not God's plan. The Rabbi and his wife had no such problem.

Meanwhile, the all-American husband, being neglected by his wife, sought fulfillment by working harder and harder. This increased tension within the marriage. His wife then, in her loneliness, began to demand not only sex but more companionship from her illicit lover. But her lover wanted only sex; so he broke off the affair.

Meanwhile, the disappointed husband turned to God. Remembering the Prophet Hosea, the husband hoped that some day his wife would put the effort into their marriage that she had put into adulterous affairs. But she was blind to her husband's goodness and blamed the husband for her unhappiness. She sought more mates, for now her rendezvous were not mere affairs but a need to rebel.

Needless to say, this all-American marriage was not the kind of happy institution it could have been if both parties had followed God's laws from the beginning of their courtship. Sin always has unforeseen and unintended results. The wife's habits made her suspicious of her husband, and she just knew he too must be unfaithful. Though she regretted her marriage, she reminded married in her sometimes miserable state because her children needed a father. To say this marriage was not what God intended is a huge understatement.

So it is with sin. Only God can fully foresee its consequences; and, in love, He gave us His law that every couple might know the bliss of the Rabbi and his wife, and avoid the grief of this all-American couple.

Both of these stories are true. Who is happier? The Rabbi and his wife were clearly ahead. The grief of the other couple – their trouble, their poor habits – actually started back when they were single, when they first committed adultery. God's laws work.

Whose Business Is It? Yet, many Americans reject this tried and true social principle: "Thou shall not commit adultery." We Americans consider sex out of wedlock a "personal affair." We have replaced God's commandment against adultery with a spurious phrase: "What two consenting adults do in private is their business."

No. It's God's business!

He has a universe to run and must think of the consequences of our behavior on others. Many buy into those ridiculous phrases without really thinking about what they are saying. Since 1960, there has been a 40% increase in the U.S. population and over a 400% increase in illegitimate births. It appears that "personal affairs" have produced many beautiful children whom God loves but who do not have the advantage of two parents as God intended.

However, two-thirds of these children will live below the poverty level. Nearly one-quarter of them will be juvenile offenders. Many of these unfortunate children will have a tough time and will suffer grief and privation of some kind. Our entire country will feel the effects and be in some degree diminished, all because of "two consenting adults."

Add to the pain of these largely unfortunate children the spread of AIDS, again usually spread by "personal affairs." In 1970, there were two kinds of venereal disease prevalent in America. Today there are at least ten, with the result that one Caucasian woman in five, and one African American woman in two, has a sexually transmitted disease. Many American marriages end in painful divorces. This is due in part to the fact that many have become so tolerant of the two-consenting-adults fantasy.

Adultery is not a victimless sin. We live with and pay the consequences of it, both in terms of quality of life and in terms of dollars of cost to our society. Sinners have always had a rationale for their sins. All we are hearing is the latest excuse for sin.

An Ominous Future? A January 1993 *Time* magazine article, entitled "Beyond the Year 2,000: What to Expect in the New Millennium," sums up the state of marriage and family in America. In the article, we find the following predictions:
- The tradition of the nuclear family will die.
- People will have multiple marriages.
- Some marriage agreements will have "sunset clauses" to terminate automatically at a given age.

- Children will often live with many different relatives.
- The taboo against incest will be broken.
- The study of the Bible will disappear.

This article should trouble every Christian. It parallels I Timothy 4:3 that prophesies a time when it will be considered in bad taste to marry. It reflects the current warped view of adultery, love, and sex prevalent in our society.

This article, along with other cultural indicators, points to the trivialization of the sacredness of holy matrimony that is occurring. These indicators should be a wake-up call for Christians everywhere to become serious about "salting the earth" and such commandments as 2 Corinthians 10:3-5:

> For though we walk in the flesh, we do not war according to the flesh. For the weapons of our warfare are not carnal but mighty in God for pulling down strongholds, casting down arguments and every high thing that exalts itself against the knowledge of God, bringing every thought into captivity to the obedience of Christ...

Marital love, duty, and honor seem to be almost forgotten values in America. A Christian marriage is far more than a civil contract. Christian love is far more lasting than simple sexual passion. Many Americans have the attitude that maintaining one's chastity is unrealistic. This is certainly different from God's Commandment against adultery.

Deceit

Bearing false witness is another prevalent sin. Bearing false witness is any action that knowingly increases the amount of misinformation in the world. Why? What harm can a little lie do? After all, free speech is constitutionally protected.

The Ubiquitous White Lie. I will explain this sin first with simple logic. We Americans constantly fall victim to false witness. False witness lurks in the small print in a contract or warrantee, the fluff or puffer in a television commercial, the spin of a politician, the defamation of a racist, and the juicy tale of a gossip. When one person bears false witness to another they mislead that person. They are attacking his or her ability to make sound decisions. Yet, we accept these kinds of misrepresentations in today's society. We do little to stop them. The Bible says that deceitfulness is an unacceptable offense, which unless repressed by the severest penalties, will destroy human society.

All That Glitters... Another example of false witness has to do with state run lotteries. Will one ticket on tonight's Big Game hurt anyone? Well it certainly will not hurt most folks. Most can afford to lose a buck. But there is another side of this.

Soon after Virginia first started its lottery, I was the vice president of operations for a manufacturing company. I recall quite vividly one young couple, 19 and 20 years old, with two small children. They were both relatively uneducated, and had entry-level jobs. Though the state clearly had the odds printed on the lottery tickets, the promise of being a millionaire by simply purchasing one of these tickets was definitely implied.

Ah, but most folks realize that this is just advertising.

This young father did not.

This beautiful little family needed every penny the couple made just to survive. The first payday after the lottery was introduced the young father stopped on the way home from work and spent his entire paycheck for lottery tickets.

I am not attacking the lottery here or this young man's lack of wisdom, or the temptation placed before him, or even the fact that it fosters gambling addiction. These are separate issues, and we are discussing deceit.

What I am attacking here is the small print on the back of lottery tickets that gives the odds of winning versus the bold, catchy, television commercial that shows lady luck driving a new car, or giving money to some happy idiot who just won a lottery. I have never seen a lottery advertisement that explained that the odds of being killed this year in an automobile accident are seven times greater than the odds of winning the lottery. I am attacking the newspaper story that tells of the man on the other side of town who won a million dollars while completely neglecting to cover people like this tragic couple who could ill afford to lose five dollars let alone half their income for two weeks. This is false witness and it has consequences.

Smoke and Mirrors. Let us look at another bit of false witness. Years after it was perfectly clear to everyone, other than those few that still believe that the world is flat, that long-term exposure to cigarette smoke would harm a person's health and even shorten life, the executives of tobacco companies still insisted that cigarettes were not habit forming. They hid their efforts to increase the addictive nature of cigarettes. They continued to oversee the use of many advertising tricks to recruit new smokers. The only difference between the tobacco executives and the folks who run the lottery is one of magnitude. Bearing false witness has consequences.

Covetousness – Contemporary Idolatry

Another example of God's law as an expression of His concern for our happiness is covetousness. Covetousness is probably the most prevalent sin in American society today. Paul equates covetousness with idolatry in at least two places (Ephesians 5:5; Colossians 3:5). While we do not see many people worshipping stone idols today, the Wall Street shrine is crowded.

Covetousness is letting our desire for power or for material wealth rule our lives. Why is this wrong? What is wrong with power? What is the harm in enjoying material wealth?

God plainly grants power to His servants. Look at Moses. However, Moses used his power righteously. That is why God chose to give him power. God wants us to have power, but to worship Him.

Look at Abraham, Isaac, and Jacob. They were all three wealthy. Abraham, Isaac, and Jacob were righteous. Their material wealth was not the governing factor in their lives. Their wealth was the result of lives well lived. Unfortunately, in our society, the desire for power and wealth often brings out the most predatory desire, the most unholy instincts and impulses we may have.

God knows that our happiness depends largely on self-control, on our ability to discipline ourselves, to make our desire for power and wealth subservient to our desire for righteousness. God knows that to be masters of our own fate, we must master our unholy desires. Discipline is the control of our baser instincts, the measure of adulthood. Without discipline, there can be no worthy life.

True strength is the control of one's passions. Strength is the absence of covetousness. Richard Nixon could have been one of America's great citizens. His desire for power cost him our country's highest office. Rather than resign, Bill Clinton did not hesitate to warp our nation's legal systems and to use the misrepresentations of the likes of James Carville to keep office. Johnnie Cochran did not see to it that O.J. Simpson got a fair trial. He used emotions and distortions to obtain fame. The covetousness of these men, their desire for power rather than their desire for righteousness, caused America much pain. Had they obeyed their Father's rules, they might have reached historical greatness beyond their dreams. However, selfishness, not God's laws, was in control of their minds.

Contrast the actions of Nixon and Clinton with those of Dr. Martin Luther King, Jr., who spoke of his willingness to die for righteousness in his last speech in Memphis the night before his assasination. We will remember Dr. King as a truly great man, a modern prophet. We will remember Nixon as a rogue. We will remember Clinton as only the second President impeached.

In many families, covetousness in the form of materialism has replaced the value of the child. Parents will work many long hours to buy a new BMW or take a Caribbean cruise rather than care properly for that most valuable of all possessions, children. The latch-key children of covetous parents get the message: Things are more valuable than people. And many of them have grown up to occupy positions of power in our society today. We pay for this.

I have to wonder if Enron executives were not children of materialism. The executives at Enron did not hesitate to hide the truth until they had sold their stock for millions. These executives prevented their employees from selling their stock until the executives broke the business. There was a time when a person did not earn an executive title unless he or she was ethical. That is obviously a bygone day. I cannot imagine that these former Enron executives fear God. When America falls, one of the reasons will be because our society has embraced the abject materialism covetousness brings.

Whether adultery, bearing false witness, covetousness, or the breach of any of His laws, God is against these sins for one reason, sin hurts us. As a nation, as a society and as individuals we suffer because we have to pass more laws and restrict more freedoms. We must hire more bureaucrats, more police officers, install more oversight commissions, and build more prisons to try to prevent behavior that godly individuals would never commit.

Furthermore, people often work their entire lives to build for retirement and then a group of unethical executives squanders their savings in an Enron-like deal. All of this means more uncertainty in our lives and more limits on our liberty and a higher tax burden for each of us. God is against sin for the same reason any father is, sinful actions have negative consequences for His children.

For the first two hundred years of our nation's existence, Judeo-Christian values were the backdrop against which America functioned. For example, God's law says,

> And if a stranger dwells with you in your land, you shall not mistreat him. The stranger who dwells among you shall be to you as one born among you, and you shall love him as yourself... (Leviticus 19:33-34).

God created all people in His image (Genesis 1:27). These and other fundamental Jewish laws shaped America's idea of equality, tolerance, and our plural society. These laws caused us to welcome immigrants, their cultures, and their thirst for freedom. However, in the last quarter of the twentieth century, Judeo-Christian ideas began getting in our secular way. For convenience, all religions have become equal with Judeo-Christian ideas. Secularism has become superior.

The Bible warns us not to be lured away from God's law and into the use of pagan law (Deuteronomy 12:30). The Bible tells us that our nation's laws should meet the minimums set by God's law, or we will go the way of the world's past great powers. In spite of this, our nation is rediscovering pagan practices and declaring them new, modern, the way thinking people should believe.

Abortion

Need more examples? What does the Bible say about abortion? Abortion on demand is an idea many defend with religious fervor. We have seen a similar secular attitude displayed in pagan cultures before. The ancient Greeks, like a number of cultures, exposed unwanted children to the elements to die. In Roman culture, life was cheap. Romans killed unwanted children. The Roman historian Tacitus deemed it a contemptible prejudice of the Jews that "it is a crime among them to kill any child!" The Jews, on the other hand, viewed little children as "the Messiahs of humankind."

In studying abortion, some interpret the Bible to permit abortion when the child inside a woman puts her life in danger. We have a duty to protect our God-given life. There appear to be no other circumstances under God's law that permit abortion.

Now my wife correctly states that Jesus tells us that we can have no greater love than to lay down our life for someone else. What I am saying is that if carrying or delivering a child puts a mother's life at risk, she may abort. However, she may also lay down her life for her child in clear conscience. Hence, as a Christian, if a woman's life is in peril by delivering a child, she still does not have a simple answer: her decision will be difficult. That is as it should be for we are dealing with human life.

A simple question clouds the abortion issue: the life of the child inside the mother, when does it start? This idea that we somehow begin life inside the mother is false. While life changes form, it is continuum. The sperm is from life and is alive; the egg is in life and is alive. The sperm and the egg unite and develop into their intended form. What we are protecting, inside the mother, is not just a life but life itself. The life in the womb is just as precious as the life outside the mother. Indeed, we have an obligation as a society to protect all lives – especially our most defenseless, our unborn children. The secular world has trouble with this view. It sees only the inconvenience the mother bears. Life is worth inconvenience.

Exodus 21: 22-23 says,

> If men fight, and hurt a woman with child, so that she gives birth prematurely, yet no harm follows, he shall surely be punished accordingly as the woman's husband imposes on him; and he shall pay as the judges determine. But if any harm follows, then you shall give life for life.

This passage says that if someone causes a woman to miscarry but the baby is born without damage, then the family has the right to compensation. The person who caused the miscarriage must pay the family for the miscarriage, the fright, the risk, the pain. If however, someone causes a woman to miscarry and that action hurts or kills the baby, the punishment's severity is equal to the damage done but not in excess of it. Unborn children have legal protection against violence; the unborn child's life is clearly equal in value to that of one born. People who perform abortions are causing the unborn child harm. Unless performed to save the mother's life, the correct charge is murder.

The Bible's rules regarding sex, if obeyed, keep people from having babies they do not want. The secular world's insistence that people have a right to have sex, whether in or out of wedlock, makes intercourse less than the sacred act God intends. This attitude turns the sex act into a sport. The secular world views human sexuality the same way it views dogs in heat: we cannot help ourselves. Nonsense! True freedom is being in control of one's passions.

In researching how the secular world caused its view on abortion to become accepted, I found it interesting that they won their "right" not through legislation, but rather through judicial maneuvering and clever marketing. In *Roe versus Wade*, the case presented to the courts had to do with the privacy rights of a mother to make her decision concerning abortion. The secular world quickly corrupted this right of privacy into abortion on demand.

The National Organization of Women (NOW) hired marketing people to help sell abortion. These people told their client that, to win their fight, NOW had to sell a woman's rights, it is her body. If, however, it appeared that life was at stake, NOW would lose the public fight. Time and precedence, and not legislative action, have now enshrined a "woman's right to an abortion." Legislative willingness to protect our unborn seems more distant every day.

Truth

The next contemporary issue I will address is truthfulness. Throughout high school, college, and graduate school, teachers and professors taught me that honest debaters avoid certain kinds of arguments. These augments, while at first appearing to be persuasive are, under closer examination, false and misleading, fallacious. Truthful people avoid fallacious arguments, for they violate logic. They are not a Christian's tools; fallacious arguments are lying. Fallacious arguments are quickly replacing logical reasoning.

Labels. Fallacious labeling is an example. There is in America a general realization that pejorative and sexist terms such as wap, kike, fag are needlessly degrading. Even words like congressman and chairman imply in a subtle but persuasive way that women are somehow inferior, that positions of power should be occupied by men. We have changed our language to minimize those negative messages. Words such as colored person have changed to African American, fireman to fire fighter and woman doctor to doctor. Now our language's subtle messages discriminate against no one – or do they?

A third grader remarked to me, "My teacher said adult movies were too violent for children to watch." I answered, "Yes." My third grade friend responded, "Why do adults like watching violence?" After that, I wonder if we are sending a subtle but persuasive message to our children when labeling things "adult." We must be an adult in order to consume adult beverages. Adult movies are our most violent and/or sexually explicit entertainment. Adult bookstores are where we go to buy our most perverted literature. Frankly, as an adult, I would just as soon not have children associate me with violence, sex, or alcohol. It would be more accurate if we called these things what they are, "violent," "sexually explicit," and "private" rather than labeling them all "adult." This fallacious label, "adult," may mislead our children into believing adulthood is about license and not about discipline.

Attack the Man. The *ad hominem* tactic is another favorite bit of fallacious reasoning rampant among politicians. The term *ad hominem* is used to express the concept of personal attacks on one's opponent rather than attacking the opponent's ideas. Since the *ad hominem* argument is usually false or irrelevant, use of it generally indicates that the person doing the attacking has weak proofs. President Clinton attacked the National Rifle Association

(NRA) as intransigent, unwilling to compromise on a single gun safety issue. The *ad hominem* assertion: Mr. Clinton claims that the NRA is responsible for much of the handgun violence in our country. Criminals are responsible for handgun violence. Few NRA members are lawbreakers. Many on the Christian right have attacked Mr. Clinton and NOW as intransigent, unwilling to compromise on a single abortion issue including late term, partial birth abortions. The *ad hominem* statement: the Christian right claims that Mr. Clinton and NOW are responsible for forty million murders. The people who made the decision to abort are responsible for those deaths. Most of these people are not members of NOW. This is America, honest differences of opinion and honest debates are not disunity; they are the vital process of making decisions in a democratic society. The truth is, the NRA, the Christian right, and NOW are simply groups of citizens who feel strongly that their position is correct and worthy of defense. Happy we should be that these groups think enough of our form of government to get involved in the process. However, with a well-informed public being necessary for a healthy America, these groups should educate us. Why do they feel their position is best for America? Any politician or group who truly believes that our system of government works should be willing to stop pretending and give us only the facts. A Christian society would demand better.

Spin. We in America have nice words for lies. Lawyers refer to "legalese" when they use gobbledygook to hide the truth. Lowly business people use "fine print" to conceal what may often be better characterized as dishonesty. Advertisers use words like "fluff" and "puffery" to describe their deceitfulness. Politicians use the word "spin" to describe their lying.

"Spin" is the subject matter of hours of television many nights in America. No matter how absurd a statement a politician makes, before the sun sets the nightly talk shows will have several guests lined up who supposedly represent each side of the issue. The nightly talk shows would have us believe that even absurd ideas must have two sides. The truth is that unscrupulous politicians know the nightly talk shows will immediately pick up a political lie and, by discussing it, give it plausibility.

The Bible teaches that lying is a serious offense against God, which unless repressed by the severest penalties, will destroy human society. To paraphrase Plato, arguments, like people, are often pretenders. Imposters and fools speak as loudly as saints and scholars. In a democratic society, it is up to the public to know enough to spot the difference. It is up to Christians to demand change.

Reasserting the Pilot Star

For the first time in American history, it is becoming unpopular to be a Christian. Rather than standing up for that which is correct in God's eyes, many Christians are bending under that pressure. I believe our failure is the cause of our society's unhappiness. A new ethic has arisen, as subversive as it is godless, which bids each man, woman or child to do that which seems right in his or her own eyes. Today, we seem to believe that all moral laws are human-made. Any law that is human-made can therefore be unmade. Things are tolerated, even encouraged, that deserve unqualified condemnation. We have lost sight of the pilot star of America's moral guidance, the Bible.

God never forces people to believe in Him. I have chosen to believe. I do not accept, I do not think of the universe as merely an aggregate of blind forces. We must not live by what is in vogue in the world but by God's laws. God is in control. The road of sanctification leads us to the happiest, most productive life possible. God's law is for the improvement, encouragement, and general benefit of those who follow it. Christ clearly calls on us to change this world – His teachings have brought out the sleeping hero in the soul of many a Christian. Will you be one? We are watching the destruction of America from within. Will you work to change the tide of events, reverse the secularization of our world?

The Bible tells us we are in a world controlled by sin. That is why we often prefer human approval to God's approval. Human beings are addicted to having what they profess to believe approved by others. The truth of what they believe often counts for little.

Untruth can be less inconvenient and more in vogue than dealing with the truth. Truth can be difficult to live with, require too much effort, and even be frightening. Therefore, taste for the truth is an acquired taste that few have the desire to develop. Untruths are too easy to come by, too quickly exploded, too cheap and fleeting to give lasting comfort, but untruths are simple, popular.

The belief in the untruth of a segregated society took hold of American for more than 100 years. So entrenched was segregation that some of our most vocal leaders defended it even as soldiers were called in to protect innocent schoolchildren from raging mobs. Still, there was the shedding of innocent blood.

New untruths have come into vogue in America. The road to sanctification requires that we study these issues, these untruths, in light of the law and not simply follow what is trendy.

Fallacious Arguments About Gay Rights

When truth won out and ended segregation in the 1960's, many Americans had to admit that they had been horribly wrong. When the gay rights issue came along, many people remembered their mistake about segregation; no one wanted to repeat such an awful error. Therefore, many self-respecting Americans did not think the issue out. Rather they jumped to say, "I support gay rights. We have learned better than to discriminate against minorities. We have grown to know the wrongness of some of the Bible's ancient teachings." The church is full of such well-meaning folks. They firmly believe the church must sanction homosexuality.

Add to this the force of peer pressure. Twenty-three hundred years ago, Aristotle said that people rarely think about what they believe in logical terms. He said people tend to believe what their peers believe.

Things have not changed. William Bryant Key, a twentieth century advertising executive, said, "No significant belief or attitude held by an individual is apparently made on the basis of consciously perceived data."

When I was in school, my psychology instructor's favorite metaphor for humans rarely questioning in-vogue opinions was the migration of the Norway Lemming. Rushing in throngs to their destination, they often press some of their companions off cliffs to fall to their deaths or into bodies of water where they drown.

8 : Major Contemporary Issues   115

The metaphor is true. We humans fail to question popularly accepted opinions. Rather, we adopt and defend these opinions looking for whatever evidence seems to support our position while discounting opposing data. We embrace trendy ideas with no clue what the results will be.

The public generally disregards what the Bible says on the issue of homosexuality. And, these people want their churches to accept their worldly views as OK. Even though the Bible speaks plainly on this subject, a number of preachers and church leaders have yielded to these same pressures and say homosexuality is indeed OK. They are asking us to believe that in this one area of a person's life, this one passion is acceptable because it is genetic. These attitudes ultimately say we trust ourselves more than we trust the Bible. Our legislators and courts ultimately protect what is in vogue in America. We are beginning to see that now. As Christians, we are about God, not about societal vogue. We are to understand and stand on what the Bible says. We are to trust God.

Many citizens read Leviticus 18:22, "Thou shalt not lie with mankind as with womankind," and say, the verse is taken out of context. They point to the laws that seem outdated. They say Moses told us not to wear clothes that contain both linen and wool. They point to the command to stone a rebellious member of society. They point to the kosher dietary rules not recognized by most Christian churches. They say that we know these rules to be wrong. They say it is the same with the rules outlawing homosexuality. They believe these rules are not only wrong; they are anti-American. They make the mistake of comparing race, a benign physiological difference, with sexual orientation, a lifestyle whose impact on society we may not yet appreciate. They believe modern ideas are superior to the notions of the ancients.

In her search for social justice, America has discovered the almost rightness of much that is wrong and the almost wrongness of much that is right.

The law as practiced around the time of Christ defined adultery, in descending order of seriousness, as: sexual relations between single people, sexual relations between people married to someone else, incest, homosexuality, and bestiality. Engaging in these practices could get one the death penalty.

In practice, the Jews have rarely applied the death penalty. God's law carries severe punishment because God wants to warn His children how risky breaking His law is for them and for their nation – not for Him – for them and for their country. God wants to discourage His children from self-destructive actions more than He wants to judge them. The Jews are about building character, not inflicting penalty. The Sanhedrin that put more than one Jew to death in "seven years, nay seventy years" considered its administration a failure – something must be wrong in Israel to let any person slip that low.

Keep in mind that the people of Moses' time, that is when God gave us the Seventh Commandment, knew first hand about the practices coming in vogue in this country today. Pagan temples often featured prostitutes, both male and female, and God hated them because they were institutions of adultery. The Prophets too, often upon pain of death, spoke out against all forms of adultery. Jesus expounded on the Ten Commandments; in every case except the law concerning the Sabbath, He tightens the rules. Jesus added that if we have lusted in our hearts, we are guilty of adultery (Matthew 5:28). It is clear that Moses, the Prophets, and Jesus viewed homosexuality, even in monogamous relationships, as inappropriate. Christians seeking sanctification must confront this issue: What does the Bible say in many places about this lifestyle?

It has been argued that homosexuality is akin to slavery – that the Bible supported slavery but we Americans have learned better. This argument is feeble. Slavery in the ancient world operated on the principle that if I could kill you but did not, then your life and all that was yours and all that would be yours was mine. Roman law did not consider slaves as alive; Egypt had similar laws. The Jews did not believe this.

The Jews did not have prisons. They often used servitude for recompense and rehabilitation. If someone broke certain laws or ran upon hard times, he or she could atone for the sin and repay the debt, thus regaining his or her status in the community, by serving as much as seven years as a servant to the person wronged. After this, the Jew reentered society. The Jews used servitude rather than jails. Consequently, the Jews had strict laws concerning the treatment of servants.

This idea is foreign to Americans. We lock up "all the bad apples" together. The Jews were about saving and rehabilitating their people – God created all people in His image – they did not want the sinner around other criminals but around righteous people. They wanted their sinners in an environment proper for retraining. God does not want to punish people. He wants them put right. Though the Jews lived in a world where slavery abounded, what they tried to practice was clearly not the kind of slavery to which the Egyptians subjected them nor that the Romans practiced. Christ, too, spoke of slavery. He taught that to change the system was to live the kind of life that would convert one's master.

In our own country, people used the Bible to support slavery but this support was fallacious. During the early 1800's abolitionists were inspired to start the Underground Railroad by Deuteronomy 23:15-16, "You shall not give back to his master the slave who has escaped from his master to you. He may dwell with you in your midst, in the place which he chooses within one of your gates, where it seems best to him; you shall not oppress him." History shows that Biblical teaching ended slavery. To portray Biblical teaching any other way seems at least ignorant, maybe a form of heresy.

Perhaps the boldest misrepresentation of truth comes from within our churches. When Christians speak out against homosexuality, we frequently hear the self-righteous indignation of some well-meaning soul say, "Let him who is without sin cast the first stone." This statement meant to correct or intimidate us only kills useful discussion. It is a ridiculous misrepresentation of Scripture.

Virtually every godly character in the Bible had faults and committed sins. We remember them because they spoke out boldly in spite of their sin. So should we. The Hebrew word for "sin" means "to miss the mark." Yes, we are all sinners. We have all missed the mark, but that is not an excuse. Christ calls on us to change the world by our love, by our actions, by our spreading God's word. He warns us of the persecutions we must face. If homosexuality is a trap, then speaking out against the sin is not self-righteousness but rather proclaiming truth. It is not trying to denigrate, it is trying to help.

Another argument frequently heard is that either you are a homosexual or you are "straight." This is probably America's weakest argument. This trendy view has little basis in fact. It is over simplistic. It overstates the effects of genetics and understates the effects of socialization.

I can imagine what my advisors from graduate school would have said if I had used such a fallacious argument: "Mr. Houston, what human skill or characteristic, be it desirable or undesirable, does not have a genetic link?"

A good friend's weight problem is probably genetic. The last time he had a physical exam his doctor told him genetics simply meant he would have to try harder than most folks to lose weight. Genetics or not, obesity will harm both the quality and the length of his life.

The ease with which people become addicted to tobacco seems to have a genetic link. Should we, on that premise, tell the smoker it is alright to smoke? Genetically caused or not, the sexual practices of homosexuals pose higher risk for one's health than does obesity or smoking. And, like smoking, it can be overcome.

The "I can't help it because it's genetic" argument is used effectively for political legitimacy. I have witnessed first hand the social agenda pushed in Washington, DC by some of our nation's richest group of lobbyists. I have spent time on the campus of a major university and seen groups of young people actively embrace the gay lifestyle. These groups pose as wanting only the recognition of monogamous same-sex relationships. Any valid look at the research available proves beyond doubt that, right or wrong, the predominant practice of gays is not monogamous; multiple partners are the rule. Sex with multiple partners is a prescription for venereal disease. Next time someone dies of a sexually transmitted disease, maybe we should write on his or her tombstone, "Here lies the victim of tolerance."

Studies of identical twins generally find against the "born gay" arguments. Genetic homosexual versus heterosexual tendencies are like IQ, they are on a continuum. Most of us have, to some

8 : Major Contemporary Issues   119

degree, a combination of tendencies. We can choose to let them govern us or not. Human sexuality is complex. Our genetic make-up is but one component. What about nurture? What are the possible effects of upbringing, training, and social environment on one's propensity to be a homosexual? Sex is the strongest drive we humans have, and thus the hardest to control. That is particularly true in young men. Now superimpose on this strong sex drive a first sexual encounter that is homosexual and you may have the first step in a powerful learning experience. Let that youth have two, three, or four homosexual experiences and some young men will have learned that homosexual experiences satisfy their most powerful drive.

Some will quickly respond that I, by using this example, am creating an alarmist hypothetical case. No, I have heard testimony from several homosexuals that that is exactly how they got into their lifestyle. God gave young men a powerful sexual drive precisely to help them overcome their bashfulness toward young women. By satisfying their sexual drive with homosexuality, we may have nurtured genetically heterosexual people into a lifestyle that will never be completely satisfying to them. Our society's current attitudes towards homosexuality are making this learned-homosexuality scenario more and more possible.

Many factors determine our sexuality. For example, with both boys and girls the father's emotional distance is a powerful determiner of sexual orientation. Situation is another determiner. Withheld heterosexual relations cause some men to try homosexual relations. Approximately 30% of prison inmates practice homosexuality of their own free will. However, many return to heterosexuality once back in society. Human sexuality is complicated, seldom determined by one factor.

I debated hard about putting this next paragraph in this book, but it needs discussing and no one seems willing to do it. Some homosexual practices are dangerous to a person's health. The most common form of sexual relations among gay men is the incretion of one man's penis in through another man's anus into his rectum. The anus and the rectum are the sewers of the human body, full of bacteria and feces. This anal insertion is often practiced in the same sexual session as is fellatio. Then there are the practices of "mud rolling" and "golden rain." How can we Americans be against cigarette smoking, for health reasons, and condone hygiene practices that guarantee harm to people's health? These practices are why gay men have shorter life spans than the general public – shorter even than smokers do.

But it is forbidden to admit this. Smokers pay increased health insurance premiums. If the insurance companies were to do the same for gay men, a cry would surely arise from special interest groups in protest. Where is the logic in all of this? Rephrasing Sir Walter Scott, "Oh what a tangled web we weave, when first we [ourselves] deceive." Gay sexual practices, like all forms of adultery, are about unbridled passion – nothing more.

Aristotle taught that people often take a position simply because it is in vogue. They argue in favor of that position even though they have not thought it out. I witnessed this in my youth in the segregated South. People openly and *en masse* defended the indefensible, the illogical, energetically; people defended segregation. A person spoke out against segregation only to his or her peril. Segregation had been around long enough to be not only people's opinion, it had become codified into law.

This is how it is becoming with homosexuality. We seem to forget that many societies have tried homosexuality only to later reject it. We disregard the health issues. We certainly are disregarding religious teachings. Then, we live in a time of unprecedented human arrogance. We are ready to try social experiments without considering the long-term consequences on our children and their society. We have just finished the bloodiest century in recorded history, and yet we think we know exactly what it takes to have a better world. We think it takes a world where God exists solely to make us feel better at funerals. God is so unimportant in American society that on Sunday mothers prefer to take their children to soccer practice rather than to church. We often hear, "I feel like I am a good person." That misses the point. The thugs that flew planes into the World Trade Center felt like they were good people. That is why God gave us the law, so that we would know what is bad for our society and us. The question is, "Do I follow God's law?"

So completely have we disguised the sexual practices of homosexuals that we rarely even recognize them as adulterous, as an abdication of the law. We Americans consider homosexuality a "personal affair." We have quickly replaced God's Commandment against adultery with a pseudo-intellectual statement from pop-culture: "What two consenting adults do in private is their business." Two consenting adults can and do agree to all kinds of poor behavior including incest – is that next on the list of accepted behaviors? I mean if a brother and sister are over eighteen and act responsibly, is not their incest their business? Who am I to condemn them? We sinners have always found seemingly rational excuses for society to accept our sins.

An argument used concerning some Roman Catholic Priests who are engaged in homosexual activity is that sexual passion is difficult to contain. While these few priests attract the media coverage, they are a small percentage of the total population of that church's leadership. The church clearly does not condone these activities.

It seems that a number of pastors and many Christians have begun the slow, almost unnoticed, slip away from God's laws and back into some form of paganism. Sounding enlightened and compassionate, some religious groups condone homosexuality. These people have made peace with the world and are bringing worldly values into the church.

This, of course, is an ancient problem. Some people have always proclaimed the righteousness of sinful actions. Jeremiah scolded Israel for that attitude, "each one chooses his own paths" (Jeremiah 8:6). The churches that accept homosexuality are saying that a great deal of what is in the Scriptures is wrong. Their decisions seem based on feelings and not upon the evidence, morality, logic, or Scripture. It is as if these churches believe that their newly-enlightened belief system is superior to God's law.

I in no way mean that homosexuals are not welcomed to attend church just as passionately as we welcome any sinner. I in no way believe that practicing homosexuals are more or less sinful than are lusting heterosexuals.

We have always worshiped beside people who are adulterous,

gossips, liars, thieves and on and on down a list of sins. We are indeed all sinners. We have all missed the mark. However, indifference to problems is more insidious than evil itself. We are too fast to forgive ourselves those sins we commit and too fast to condemn sinners we do not understand. We are too fast to condemn the public sins of others and to hide our own private sins. If we have the power to help anyone in need and do not, we are less than Christ's followers. Homosexuality, even that which is monogamous and hidden, is adultery. Thus, it is something every Christian on his or her way to sanctification must strive to change.

At this writing, I reside in Vermont. Vermont was the first state to permit civil unions. As the result of this law, many gays and lesbians have come to this beautiful state. I work with some of these people. They are fine citizens. I have close relatives who are homosexual. I love these relatives. The friendships and love I share with these people made me well understand their desire for social acceptance. I remember Moses and Abraham debating God about some of His decisions. Debating this subject is acceptable and understandable. Remember when addressing this issue in debate that God's laws are all about leading more fulfilling lives. His law restricts our passion for the best of reasons. God wants people to come to Christ and then begin the process of sanctification. God's word says homosexuals will be happier, lead more fulfilling lives, if they change their lifestyle. We will each lead happier more fulfilling lives if we identify our sins, renounce them and change.

The Aversion to Change

Most people do not want to deal with sin. No one wishes to admit that, "I have missed the mark." They have not so much tried Christianity and found it wanting as they have known it is difficult and left it untried. They want to feel good about themselves and ignore serious change. When people came to Jesus and asked what they must do to be faithful to Him, He rarely said, "simply believe." Jesus said, "Follow me." "Follow me" means to change one's attitude toward self, toward sin, and toward God's laws – all of them. Jesus asks us not to be lukewarm Christians (Revelation 3:16). Being Christian requires total commitment.

There was a time not many years ago when grandma, grandpa, aunts, uncles, and cousins were a few miles away. Andy Griffith's Mayberry was more than a tale. Everyone in a community knew and cared about everyone else. Technology and transportation have weakened the extended family, undermined communities that once supported us. Today many of us feel alone in life. Our world-view has shifted toward being self-centered. We feel less responsible for others and less secure as a result. Once taken for granted as right, people now fear that they will be considered unintelligent if they raise any opposition to sexual sins. Christ calls on us not to be afraid of popular opinion or of being condemned.

I ask if Matthew 15:8-9 is applicable today? Christ said,

> These people draw near to Me with their mouth, And honor Me with their lips, But their heart is far from Me. And in vain they worship Me, Teaching as doctrines the commandments of men.

It is so much easier, it is far more socially acceptable, to follow man-made teachings than it is to follow God's law. Should we stand up against the popular culture, or should we support it? What is correct in God's eyes? The answer is obvious.

So long as we relinquish nothing, it is easy to be Christian. Christianity is easy as long as our church says all that is worldly is good, not to be condemned. However, if we stand with the popular culture, we are scoffing at the holiness of purity. We have lost sight of the sacredness of the human dignity gained through self-discipline. Our culture is leaving us at the mercy of unbridled gratification, of impulses that civilized humankind once taught that we must control. We are dethroning God in the sphere of human conduct, derided moral inhibitions. We have declared instinct and inclination to be the true guides to human happiness.

Good and evil, once as distinguishable as day and night, have become a blurred mist. But this mist is man-made. God is not silent; we are simply failing to listen. There are absolute truths. Jumping off the Empire State Building is a dangerous thing regardless of your opinion on the subject. Einstein's theory of relativity does not imply relativism. On the contrary, it assumes that there are absolutes. Individuals and groups who think they can make up morality, as if their minds wholly determine right and wrong, need mental help. The Ten Commandments are not The Ten Suggestions.

I believe that Biblical prophecy is similar to biblical history; while it may record the events of a specific time, its lessons are valuable reading all the time. Some pastors believe that I and II Timothy are particularly applicable to our country today. The prophecies in I and II Timothy have to do with many people in the church falling away from the teachings of Christ and with people embracing false teachings, false doctrine.

> For the time will come when they will not endure sound doctrine, but according to their own desires, because they have itching ears, they will heap up for themselves teachers; and they will turn their ears away from the truth, and be turned aside to fables (II Timothy 4:3-4).

The words in I and II Timothy are a communication, a warning, to us that we are on the path of moral depravity. We are going down a path that misses and destroys those things in life that make it truly wonderful. As for the path our country is on, there is a stronger warning; Isaiah 5:20-21 says,

> Woe to those who call evil good, and good evil; Who put darkness for light, and light for darkness; Who put bitter for sweet, and sweet for bitter! Woe to those who are wise in their own eyes, And prudent in their own sight!

Unlike modern Americans, Jesus has no misunderstanding of reality. He understands God's perfect plan for humankind. He calls us through the narrow gate to perfection. Like a young child, who hasn't developed a firm sense of past and future, His teachings are about the abundance of the present, the abundance of a life found in trusting, in following God's law completely. I firmly believe that if Jesus were to come back and walk among men and women today that He would visit gay bars and bathhouses. But, He would call homosexuals away from this destructive lifestyle to repentance and forgiveness (Luke 5:32).

Simultaneously, Jesus would be condemned as homophobic, erroneously so because He would rebuke homosexuality as sin. He might also be called alcoholophobic, drugophobic, and maybe even tobaccophobic.

8 : Major Contemporary Issues

Jesus would want us to help Him treat destructive illnesses and addictions. And so we should. Christ calls on us to reprove sin, to convert those who are in pain. In this kind of conversion, we must have humility. We must treat those with whom we disagree with an extra portion of respect and affection; we must be both critical and friendly at the same time. This is difficult. It has a price. "Therefore let those who suffer according to the will of God commit their souls to Him in doing good, as to a faithful Creator" (I Peter 4:19).

God Confirms the Law

Many Christians think the law has been superceded, but that is far from the truth, as the following references show:

> Now after six days Jesus took Peter, James, and John his brother, led them up on a high mountain by themselves; and He was transfigured before them. His face shone like the sun, and His clothes became as white as the light. And behold, Moses and Elijah appeared to them, talking with Him. Then Peter answered and said to Jesus, "Lord, it is good for us to be here; if You wish, let us make here three tabernacles: one for You, one for Moses, and one for Elijah." While he was still speaking, behold, a bright cloud overshadowed them; and suddenly a voice came out of the cloud, saying, "This is My beloved Son, in whom I am well pleased. Hear Him!" And when the disciples heard it, they fell on their faces and were greatly afraid. But Jesus came and touched them and said, "Arise, and do not be afraid." When they had lifted up their eyes, they saw no one but Jesus only (Matthew 17:1-8).

Here God Himself declares Jesus His Son and here God also confirms the importance of Moses and Elijah, the law and the prophets. This experience means we should listen to Christ and to those whom God sent before Him.

In Acts 9:1-20, Christ calls Paul to be His Apostle. This certainly implies that we should listen to Paul. Paul's writings give us new insights into the law and the prophets.

> What shall we say then? Is the law sin? Certainly not! On the contrary, I would not have known sin except through the law... (Romans 7:7).

Paul's writings tell us that we are not born knowing what is good or bad for us, what is sin. Paul's writings tell us that societies often sanction certain sins. For those reasons, God wrote His law. Christ's life is our example.

Every person eventually has to make a choice: either the law defines what is good or bad or society does. Do we believe in the law, the Prophets, Christ and both Testaments or are there mistakes? On the one extreme, there are people who interpret the Bible literally; they see the Bible as the inerrant Word of God. On the other extreme are people who see the Bible as simply a religious book full of myths – interesting, but totally of human origin. Then there are many people who position themselves somewhere between the two extremes. So, where are you?

> Not everyone who says to Me, "Lord, Lord," shall enter the kingdom of heaven, but he who does the will of My Father in heaven (Matthew 7:21).

This is stated another way in Revelation 3:15-16:

> I know your works, that you are neither cold nor hot. I could wish you were cold or hot. So then, because you are lukewarm, and neither cold nor hot, I will vomit you out of My mouth.

In your attempt at sanctification, are you hot, cold, or lukewarm?

9 : Forgiving: For Growth and a Free Mind

> *During the past thirty years,*
>   *people from all the civilized countries of the earth*
>   *have consulted me.*
> *I have treated many hundreds of patients....*
> *Among all my patients of the second half of my life –*
>   *this is to say, over thirty-five [years] –*
>   *there has not been one whose problem in the last resort*
>   *was not that of finding a religious outlook on life....*
>   —Dr. Carl Jung

Not too long after my twenty-second birthday, I arrived in Viet Nam, a machine-gunner in the 199th Light Infantry Brigade. Seven days later, I experienced my first combat. From that day forward I wrote each letter home with care, for I suddenly knew that it might be the last words my family would receive.

Last Words

A person's last words can be revealing. Karl Marx's ideas put many nations on the horrible road to communism. On the day Karl Marx died, March 14, 1883, his housekeeper came to him and said, "Mr. Marx, tell me your last words, and I'll write them down." Marx replied, "Go, get out! Last words are for fools who haven't said enough!" P.T. Barnum, the founder of Barnum and Bailey's Greatest Show on Earth, asked as he was dying, "What are the receipts of the day?" Napoleon's last words were, "I am Chief of the Army!" The great Baptist preacher, Charles Spurgeon's last words were, "Jesus died for me." And, Charles Wesley, the initiator of the Methodist Church, said, "Best of all is, God is with us."

Jesus' Last Words. The Bible records seven last statements that Christ uttered while He was on the cross. These statements are important to us, not only because Jesus spoke them, but also because of the place where He said them. While Christ was on the cross, He was doing His greatest work; He was uttering some of His greatest words. Luke records some of the last words of Jesus. Listen to them, "Then said Jesus, 'Father, forgive them; for they know not what they do'" (23:34).

Sometimes it is difficult for us to forgive people. Someone hurts us, someone says something against us and, in our hearts, we cannot forgive that person. Listen to Jesus' prayer, "Father, forgive them; for they know not what they do." Jesus spoke these words of forgiveness in behalf of the people who only the day before had shouted, "Crucify Him!" Jesus spoke these words of forgiveness in behalf of the people who, only minutes before, had nailed Him to the cross. Notice the wonder of His words. Christ's words reflect a world-changing attitude.

I hear Christians say, "I cannot talk to God! I cannot pray! I do not believe anymore – after the way people have treated me."

Look at the way people treated Jesus. He had preached love. He had healed the sick. He had fed the poor. He had done nothing bad to anyone. His only crime was to upset the social order. For this, His nation sinned against Him.

His own disciples failed Him and fled. Peter denied Him. He was up all night, being dragged from one kangaroo court to

9 : Forgiving: For Growth and a Free Mind

another, and was found guilty of crimes He did not commit. He was beaten almost beyond recognition, thorns stuck into His head, made to drag His own cross, spikes driven through His hands and feet, raised up on the cross, and suspended by His nail torn flesh between two thieves to suffer death. But still He said, "Father forgive them."

Trusting His Father's Love. In spite of all this, Jesus was able to look up into the heavens and begin His prayer with, "Father." He lived in fellowship with his Father, and knew that even under these horrible circumstances His Father loved Him. I remember in Matthew chapter 22, verses 34 through 37 when the Pharisees asked Jesus, "Teacher, which is the great commandment in the law?" and "Jesus said to him,'You shall love the LORD your God with all your heart, with all your soul, and with all your mind.'" Jesus, under these most difficult circumstances of His life remained true to His Father, never doubting God's love even while nailed to the cross.

Perhaps you are hurting now. You are thinking, "If God loves me how can He let me suffer so." God loved Jesus and yet He was willing to see Jesus die a horrible death. No matter how bad things seem, God loves us and He always will; of that have no doubt. Do not lose faith. He is working out His purpose for each of us. Christ's agony on that cross was for the greatest purpose. God raised Him to eternal glory.

It is not easy to suffer. Pain hurts. It seems so unfair. A broken heart hurts far worse than a broken arm. If we really want to be a sanctified Christian, Jesus, here on the cross, shows us where we must start. We must start by following God's will no matter if our circumstances seem as dark as those that Jesus faced on the cross that day two thousand years ago. When we can say, "Father," then we are able to look up to heaven and know that God will make all right.

Forgive Them. Next in Christ's appeal we find "forgive them." "Father, forgive them." A tradition indicates that our Lord repeated this prayer several times. He said it as they laid Him on the cross as it lay on the ground. He said it as they drove the spikes through His flesh. He said it as they raised His cross, its base sliding into a hole in the ground, jerking erect with a sudden and painful thud. And, finally, He said it as He hung there dangled in the air by His mangled meat. "Father, forgive them."

Seeing it Through. He could have prayed, "Father, judge them; Father, bring punishment upon them." He could have called down legions of angels to deliver Him, but He did not. The thing that kept Christ on that cross was love, not nails.

I repeat, the thing that kept Christ on that cross was love, not nails. Jesus knew what was going to happen to Him. He knew He was going to the cross. Remember Luke 22:21 records what Jesus said the night before He was betrayed at the Last Supper, "But behold, the hand of My betrayer is with Me on the table." Christ told Judas to go do what he had to do.

Remember when Jesus went to the Garden of Gethsemane to pray before Judas showed up with the Temple guards. Jesus could have run. I read portions from Luke 22:39-46, "Coming out, He went to the Mount of Olives, as He was accustomed, and His disciples also followed Him. When He came to the place…He was withdrawn from them about a stone's throw, and He knelt down and prayed, saying, 'Father, if it is Your will, take this cup away from Me; nevertheless not My will, but Yours, be done'…And being in agony, He prayed more earnestly. Then His sweat became like great drops of blood falling down to the ground…."

Jesus knew what was coming. He had the power to turn and run away from the horrible pain that He knew the Romans would inflict on Him and yet He said, "not My will, but Yours [Father] be done." Jesus went to the cross because He loved us. He went to the cross knowing that He would pray "Father, forgive them."

Many times some of us may have wanted to bring down fire from heaven on someone, and wanted to pray, "Father, judge them for their sin against me." But, our Lord gave us His example that day: "Father, forgive them."

Christ practiced the message that He preached. He preached forgiveness. He told His people in His messages, "Now, if you do not forgive from your heart, God cannot forgive you." This does not mean that the basis of forgiveness is our own good works. No, but it does mean that if in our hearts we are unwilling to forgive others, we are in no condition to come and ask God for forgiveness for ourselves. Let me repeat that: If we are unwilling to forgive others, we are in no shape to enter into God's presence and ask for forgiveness. Forgiveness of a wrong against us is a form of mastering ourselves, of moving to Christlikeness.

A World Seeking Revenge. We must remember that all of this happened while Rome ruled the world. The Romans worshipped revenge. Revenge was one of their gods. Revenge is the god of the terrorists that flew airplanes full of innocent people into the Twin Towers murdering 3,000 people who God created in His image. Our Lord Jesus did not worship revenge, nor should we. He prayed, "Father, forgive them." In doing so, He fulfilled the Word. He practiced His own message of forgiveness.

This, of course, was the purpose of His death. Our Lord was on the cross so God could justly forgive sinners. That is the message of the Gospels. We do not have to go around with the weight and burden of anger and revenge on our lives. We do not have to carry the guilt of sin. We can forgive!

The Message of the Cross

Forgiveness is the message of the cross. Forgiveness is not cheap; it is very expensive. It cost Jesus His life. We will have no problem forgiving others if we are right in our relationship with our Father, and remember that God has forgiven us.

Those who do not forgive others tear down the bridge on which they themselves will have to walk. Romans chapter 3, verse 23, "for all have sinned and fall short of the glory of God." God loves us. We are rebellious, we act selfishly, we are immoral, we sin, yet God loves us intensely. He loves us beyond anything that we can comprehend. He loves us so much that He gave His only Son, Jesus the Christ, to die on that cross.

Jesus was able to say, "Father, forgive them; for they know not what they do." Our Lord not only prayed for forgiveness of His enemies, but with this last phrase, He argued on their behalf. It is as though He stood as a lawyer and said to His Father, "Let me give you a reason why you should forgive them. They know not what they do. They are ignorant of the enormity of their actions.

They do not realize what great sinners they are." Jesus was saying in effect, "Father, my people do not understand. They do not know that I am dying for them. They know not what they do. I know what I am doing; I am dying for them. Now, Father, forgive them that I will not have died in vain." And even in this most horrible of circumstances, He set a final example.

The early New Testament Scriptures, written mostly in Greek, commonly used the word *aphesis* to convey the English, "forgiveness." *Aphesis* means, "sending away" or "letting go." Quite simply put, "Father, forgive them; for they know not what they do" is letting go. It is the understanding of the basic fact that good is permanent, always present, and all-powerful. Evil is temporary, insubstantial and without its own character. The trick is the proper spiritual treatment of evil. Do not wrestle with evil. Not to forgive a wrong done to us is to give further life and power to that evil. How foolish. Evil cannot come into our life unless there is something in us with which it is attuned. By forgiving that wrong, not only do we remove its ability to do us more harm, we present the wrongdoer with an example that may change him or her.

Paul covers this point quite well:

> Repay no one evil for evil. Have regard for good things in the sight of all men. If it is possible, as much as depends on you, live peaceably with all men. Beloved, do not avenge yourselves...for it is written, "Vengeance is Mine, I will repay," says the Lord. Therefore "If your enemy is hungry, feed him; If he is thirsty, give him a drink; For in so doing you will heap coals of fire on his head." Do not be overcome by evil, but overcome evil with good (Romans 12:17-21).

God wants us to be happy. Christ was still thinking only of us and our happiness there on the cross. His final words about forgiving even those who have horribly wronged us are a part of our guide to the happiness God wants for us. When we will not forgive someone, we are expressing a degree of hate. That hate has negative psychological and physiological effects on us. Hatred is one of the most destructive of emotions. Indeed, every time we think about something someone did to us, we relive whatever reason we think we have for hating him or her. We become the victim of our own thoughts.

That is one reason why we are not to bear a grudge or seek vengeance. I mean, even though someone has harmed us in some way, every time we remember that harm or seek vengeance or bear a grudge, we relive the pain. In our minds, we become victims again. Our emotions do not allow us to differentiate between the real and the imagined. Only by removing the hatred, through forgiveness, do we release the pain and remove the ability of the person or group to keep hurting us again and again. Forgiveness means we no longer victimize ourselves.

This reliving of our victimhood is one reason why God forbids us to seek vengeance. We shall not repay evil with evil. We are to return good for evil (Matthew 5:43-48). Jesus says that in so doing maybe we will make an enemy into a friend. Only forgiveness removes our sin of hatred.

By forgiving, we remove the ability of that wrong to do us more harm. Forgiveness is for our happiness; forgiveness is God's mercy on us, the victim of a wrong. Forgiveness breaks the cycle and lets us get on with our life. Forgiveness removes us from victim status.

"Father, forgive them; for they know not what they do." Again, I say, nails did not hold Jesus on the cross, love did. Jesus' last words from the cross gave us an example of how we may join Christ in His work on earth. These last words show us how to slip from evil's hold on our lives. Jesus, while suffering to death on the cross, showed us another way to help establish His Kingdom on Earth.

We have a complete Bible from Adam to Christ's second coming. We are not ignorant of the requirement that as Christians we must forgive all who have sinned against us. We are not to carry revenge in our hearts. It will hurt us much more than it will hurt the ones who wronged us. God is patient with us that we may have time to be reconciled both with God and with ourselves. And He asks us to treat others the same way. Is that too much?

My request of you is that you honor Jesus' last words, search your heart. Is there someone you hate so much that for you to meet him or her on the street is to suffer? Is there someone who has you in victim status? Is there someone whom you need to forgive? If there is, know that Christ wants you free of your pain: forgive! Forgive that you may do what Christ would have you do. Forgive that you may enjoy life better. Forgive that you may join Christ in establishing His way as your way.

Seeking Forgiveness

Now that we have covered our obligation to forgive others, we must cover our obligation to seek forgiveness from others. Both are a part of the sanctification process.

God is compassionate, kind, and righteous. He wants only what is best for us. He has no ulterior motives. We are His children. As children, we are bound to fail as we grow, as we mature. God wants our failures to be a time of growth. Therefore, when we do fail, our Father wants us to renounce the missed mark. He wants us to make good any harm we have done. He wants us to think how we will act differently next time. These things – remorse, seeking forgiveness, and renewal – are the process of repentance, another part of sanctification's process of growth.

Seems simple enough, but the average Christian practices a false or, what I call, a feel-good-self-forgiveness. A person sins, and they utter a little prayer saying "Father, please forgive me." They think that that is enough – minimal remorse, no seeking forgiveness from the aggrieved party, no renewal, no growth and no good – this is self-deception. We cannot forgive ourselves of a wrong done God; God has to do that. We cannot forgive ourselves of a wrong done to another human being; while God can do this, as Christians, we need to seek the forgiveness of the person we may have wronged. It is straightforward, logical, but too often embarrassment and pride cause us to miss the opportunities for growth this process of repentance offers.

We are hung up on success, on appearances. We miss these chances for development. Proverbs talks about getting things wrong and learning from our mistakes, "My son, do not despise the chastening of the LORD, Nor detest His correction; For whom the LORD loves He corrects, Just as a father the son in whom he delights" (Proverbs 3:11-12). "Whoever loves instruction loves knowledge, But he who hates correction is stupid" (Proverbs 12:1).

9 : Forgiving: For Growth and a Free Mind

Seeking forgiveness is accepting rebuke and discipline. Seeking forgiveness is about growing, about being the best we can be.

Repentance: The Condition for Forgiveness. Prior to discussing forgiveness further, it is necessary to discuss sin. I see no need to emphasize what others have said about sin. Rather, I want to emphasize a less-talked-about understanding. God our Father has conditions that we must meet. These conditions have one end, that we might lead better lives. It does not take much imagination for even the most unreligious to realize that if all people obeyed God's law the world would be a much safer, better place.

Sin ranges from simple lies to self-indulgent lifestyles to what Adolph Hitler did – sin is living by our rules rather than by God's rules. Sin is giving in to our animal impulses rather than learning to "love thy neighbor as thyself."

Godly Sorrow (2 Corinthians 7:10). The persons who are attempting to have God's law written on their heart must understand the infinite forgiveness available from God. The act of seeking forgiveness is repentance toward God and faith in Christ.[1]

---

[1] Maybe the following little discourse on repentance, by one I count as a friend, will be of some value to those who read this book:

"Biblically, repentance is a universal prerequisite for forgiveness. Over 60 times it is so demanded in the New Testament and many times in the Old Testament. That is true especially our initial reconciliation to God for salvation. It is also true for the individual sins we commit afterward, if we are conscious of them and are thus convicted in our hearts about them.

"Initially, in every person who is genuinely saved, repentance is a deep response growing out of real contrition concerning all sin as a principle (2 Cor. 7:10, 11; Psalm 51:17; Acts 3:19; Luke 13:5, and many more). Even though we could never recall every specific sin or remember them all, still the believer hates sin as lawlessness (1 John 3:4).

"Since Christ, on the cross, has legally propitiated all our sin – past present and future, known or unknown – He forgives all; and from that time forward the true believer is not under law but grace. And because of this grace, O happy condition, the law does not condemn the soul of the believer (Rom. 5:20; 6:14). "Nevertheless, it is still right, our privilege and great advantage, to obey the law (Rom. 6:15); for sin enslaves, destroys life and joy, and brings reproach upon the name of God.

"Therefore we need sanctification – to repent of each sin, and to rehabituate our conduct in righteousness. For now, as we see sin in our lives, it grieves the penitent heart; and repentance is the spontaneous response of a

Repentance and faith are inseparable graces (Acts 20:21), a single religious act – the exercise of both a God-given privilege and a duty. For the people performing this duty, God provides not only forgiveness but once we are saved, He provides growth.

Seeking forgiveness is the result of feeling sin's effect and grieving about it – a sorrow toward God that we have let Him down – realizing that what we are doing is wrong for His world and for ourselves. It is saying we do not want that anymore. Then we must go to God and beg Him, often with tear-filled eyes, to forgive us. Further, we do our best to undo the problems we have caused. Now we must change. We want so badly not to live outside of God's law that, when faced with the same situation again, we do not repeat that mistake. When we come to Him with a broken heart, we know that He forgives us of that particular sin (Psalm 51:17).

Restitution. Finally, we work to inform others or, better, work to eliminate the kind of situation that tempted us to sin. This, as far as possible, is to make things right again and so that others will not fall into the same trap in which we once found ourselves. As this last step occurs, we are participating with God in His creative process of sanctification.

When Sin Goes Public. Seeking and receiving forgiveness from other humans is similar to seeking forgiveness from God. Seeking forgiveness from God is a private affair. However, seeking forgiveness from a fellow human being can be painfully public. When dealing with God who will forgive us "seven times seventy" (Matthew 18:21-22), it is easier. We are dealing with a God who will "remove our sins as far as the east is from the west" (Psalm 103:12). We are dealing with a God who "will remember our sins no more" (Jeremiah 31:34).

But when we are dealing with people, sinners, who are just regenerate heart as Scripture trains our sensitivity to sin.

"Moreover, repentance on the part of those who have sinned against us or others is a condition for our forgiveness of them (Lk. 17:3, 4). But even if they don't seek our forgiveness, that doesn't mean we hate them even as God does not hate the unrepentant sinner *per se*; He pities them.

"To not repent, which is a heart-felt change of mind and attitude toward sin, is to retain the sin in the heart. Therefore, God will not take the impenitent into His heaven (Luke 13:3), for no sin shall enter there."

9 : Forgiving: For Growth and a Free Mind

as fallible as we are, it can be much more difficult. For example, people with whom I have worshipped have said some mean things about me. These people have never sought my forgiveness. We have all witnessed our fellow Christians offend other members of their church. We witness repentance only from the most devout. Even good people have a hard time with seeking forgiveness from others.

I remember one woman in a church I attended who was a gossip. We had a preacher she did not care for. When he moved to another church this woman sent the pastor's new church a clipping from a newspaper. The clipping reported some trouble this preacher's wife had encountered. A storeowner had accused her of shoplifting. Now obviously this article caused the pastor and his wife pain. A pastor's job, supported by his wife, is difficult enough without someone trying to make the thing not work.

Now, if this woman had truly been sorry for what she did, the proper approach to repentance would have been something like this: first, this repentant woman should have gotten on her knees and begged God to forgive her. Second, she would have asked for forgiveness from the pastor and his wife. In this case, appearing in person would have been appropriate. Third, the repentant woman should have gotten up in front of the pastor's new church and apologized. She should have given his new congregation reasons why they should accept the new pastor and his wife as their own. Fourth, the repentant woman should have gotten up in front of her church and apologized for any bad light she brought upon it. Finally, the repentant woman should have tried to help the pastor and his wife at their new church.

Now you may not completely agree with my recommendations and that is fine, but you get the idea. Gossip is serious sin. It violates Leviticus 19:16. Repenting of gossip is a troublesome matter; it has to elicit real change. Had the gossiping woman taken these steps, I do believe the humiliation she brought upon herself would have cured her of future gossiping. As it was, she simply showed up at church the Sunday after this incident became public knowledge and continued in her ways. May God have more mercy on her than she had on others.

A Word on Damage Control. Not all sins offer as much opportunity for growth. Obviously, not all sins affect as many people as this sin of gossip did. Seeking forgiveness is not always as public and humiliating. Lying often affects only one or two people. Stealing, unless from a large organization, often affects only a few people. When fewer people are involved, seeking forgiveness is less public, and thus less time and effort are involved.

The more people sinned against, the larger the consequences of the sin, the more public the sin, the more work required to repair the damage done, and the more humiliating is the whole matter. However, the requirements of admitting fault, making good the damage done, and begging forgiveness are all part of the process of repentance and restitution regardless of the size or severity of the sin.

What about sins where the victim is no longer around? The victim has moved to an unknown place, or the sin is murder or causing a deadly accident, how does one ask a missing or a dead person for forgiveness? Obviously, it cannot be done. Yet, the obligation of admitting fault, and undoing as much of the damage as is possible, still remains. This includes taking care of the victim's family and helping the victim's friends. All persons we sin against must hear, "please forgive me." Otherwise, we are forgetting a victim; we are being pitiless.

Keep in mind the purpose of the repentance process. It is a duty before God, but it is also growth. It is about change. What we want is a permanent change in ourselves and thus an improvement in our world. We want to stop sinning. We want to become more Christlike. The fear of having to repent itself is a deterrent for the devout person.

Should You Demand Forgiveness? What about the aggrieved person or persons against whom you have sinned? Is your duty to seek their forgiveness conditional upon their willingness to forgive you? By no means! Even though they are commanded to forgive those who seek forgiveness (Luke 17:3, 4), if they do not, that's none of your affair. Your duty to seek forgiveness from them derives from God, regardless of how they respond.

Remember that forgiveness would not be necessary if the sin had not been committed in the first place. Most works I have read say that you should approach the wronged party sincerely seeking forgiveness. Now, Christ wants everyone to forgive quickly and easily. However, the aggrieved person does not have to forgive us. The belligerence of the victim of our sin is not the issue here. Producing a change in the sinner is the issue. If a sincere approach does not produce the words, "I forgive you," leave it to God.

Every Waking Moment. The only step in the Christian life in Christ more fundamental than growth – attempting to do God's will and seeking forgiveness as we fail – is our initial response to God to "repent, and believe the Gospel" (Mark 1:15). The Bible refers to your initial plea for forgiveness as being "saved," "born again" or "regeneration," being "justified by faith." God's response to your broken-hearted repentance for all your sins and your faith in His full payment for them on the cross, is sometimes called "eternal life," which refers not merely to duration but to quality as well.

Then, as a "new creation" in Christ, the second step involves the truth that following God's law and hence seeking forgiveness when you fail becomes a part of your every waking moment. That aspect of the true Christian life is the inevitable extension of the Christian's original repentance and faith – his penitent spirit and love of God's law which has been put in his heart by regeneration – thus the pursuit of sanctification in his personal life is as natural to a new Christian as nursing is to a baby. And it's a great pity that too often pastors, churches, or more mature Christians fail to show the new-born ones the source of nourishment.

A Solemn Warning. Both Mark 3:29 and Matthew 12:32 tell us that there is one sin God will not forgive, blasphemy against the Holy Spirit. Saint Augustine understood this to mean deliberate persistence in doing evil. Passages such as Matthew 18:33-35, Hebrews 6:4-8; and 10:26-29 imply that both an unrepentant spirit and, its corollary, an unforgiving spirit are at the root of this desolate condition.

Why?

Why does God single out one sin as unpardonable – "neither in this world, neither in the world to come"?

If a person neither feels remorse for sin nor desires forgiveness, that person cannot repent, and it is the pre-salvation work of the Holy Spirit to convict, to illuminate, and to draw the sinner to Christ (compare John 16:8; Hebrews 6:4-6; John 6:44, 65). But if the sinner, with all that illumination of the Gospel and drawing by God in the Person of the Holy Spirit, turns blasphemously against the very Person doing the drawing, then the Holy Spirit withdraws from Him, leaving him forever in his darkness.

That person is calling evil good and good evil: "Woe to those who call evil good, and good evil; Who put darkness for light, and light for darkness; Who put bitter for sweet, and sweet for bitter!" (Isaiah 5:20).

That person is blaspheming the Holy Spirit, and he or she forfeits all – both salvation and the priceless experience and opportunity to grow, to walk with God and know the joy of His fellowship and blessings.

However, it is not God's decision. The sinner in his blasphemy rejects, once and for all, the very Spirit who liberates the will. That is, the hard-core sinner does not desire forgiveness; his lot is set. "Ephraim is joined to idols, Let him alone" (Hosea 4:17).

The Beauty of Holiness. God is about truth and justice, and so we should be. God is merciful, and so we should be. God is full of kindness and forgiveness, and so we should be. The process of repentance for sins against God and against our fellow human beings, humanly speaking, is a difficult process. But the process was put in place by our Heavenly Father. He loved us so much that He wants us to develop into the best we can be.

He asks us to change the world. If we are going to do that, we must not be afraid to face anyone because of a mistake we made against them or even against Him. How beautiful is the world He wants us to live in. Not only should we seek to forgive quickly and often, I think Christ would have us end each day with a prayer that includes the following phrase, "God forgive those who sinned against me today, I already did." Stated more formally, "And forgive us our debts, As we forgive our debtors" (Matthew 6:12).

We are too often content to wallow in the sinful pleasures of the world, to trust more in ourselves than in God. God participates in, feels, the suffering of our world. He has given us tools to change the world. God wants us to forgive others. He also wants us to repent, to make the evil in the world improve. The repentance process is powerful. Christians arise. Do your duty. Change the world into the Garden of Eden God intended. Use this process. Grow. Discover the bounty God wants you to have.

10 : The Principle of Giving

"Will a man rob God? Yet you have robbed Me!...
In tithes and offerings....
Bring all the tithes into the storehouse...
And try Me now in this...
If I will not open for you the windows of heaven
and pour out for you such blessing
that there will not be room enough to receive it."
—Malachi 3:8–10

Obviously, God does not need our money. He does not need us to help Him do His good works. God created the universe and its billions of galaxies. He owns them. God does not need anything we have. Yet Malachi conveys God's demand that we share what we have with others.

God could give others what He has given us. Why does He assign us that duty? In His infinite generosity, He created us in His image. Out of all the wealth of His universe, He gave us His garden, this world, and asked us to tend it. Nothing pleases Him more than for us to join Him in His work. Sharing what God has given us is living in His image. It is reproducing, replicating, and multiplying His love through our actions. It puts us in rhythm with His creation.

Further, Malachi conveys a powerful promise for those who satisfy their duty. The ability to donate is a gift from our Father. Tithing, giving and doing good works are not for God's good but for our good. In a giving society, community, or church, we need not fear; our neighbors are as ready to help us as we are ready to help them. This attitude assures us all that those in need will have all they require. This sharing the wealth is doing unto others as we would have others do unto us. Sharing the wealth enriches everyone materially and spiritually. Giving ensures that the harvest of our lives will be rich and abundant.

The Tithe

Fundamental to the principle of giving is the tithe. Ten percent of our income, our tithe, is the minimum we must give. The history of this goes back at least to Abram. In Genesis 14:17-24 we find that Abram, after rescuing Lot, meets with Melchizedek, the king of Salem and a priest of God Most High, and Abram gives Melchizedek ten percent of his wealth. Later, in Genesis 28:20-22, we see the concept of tithing become the rule for God's people.

> Then Jacob made a vow, saying, "If God will be with me, and keep me in this way that I am going, and give me bread to eat and clothing to put on, so that I come back to my father's house in peace, then the LORD shall be my God. And this stone which I have set as a pillar shall be God's house, and of all that You give me I will surely give a tenth to You" (Genesis 28:20-22).

In this time of the Patriarchs, God was entitled to share directly in livestock, grain, wine, and oil that a family produced.

Tithing Codified as Law. We find in Deuteronomy that in the time of Moses, tithing became law. It was for the support of the Levites, Priest, aliens, the fatherless, widows and helping others. Further, we find there were actually several occasions that required a tithe. There were specific instructions concerning the firstborn of the flocks and the fruits of the fields. Pilgrims brought these items to Jerusalem for distribution. If the trip to Jerusalem was too far, pilgrims sold the goods for money. They took the money to Jerusalem and converted it back into goods. The priest, strangers, widows, and orphans shared these provisions. Every third year the provisions stayed in their local community. During the exile period, the local Levite received the tithe. We are not living in the agricultural times of the Patriarchs, but the rules are the same: God commands us to tithe ten percent of our property and produce for His ministers, churches and taking care of the needy.

More Blessed to Give. We are required to give according to our means, but we are to give even if we have only a little. The widow's offering as presented in Luke 21:1-4 tells us it is not the amount. It is the giving heart. Jesus said, "it is more blessed to give than to receive" (Acts 20:35). Anyone who has purchased a gift for a poor child for Christmas, given an indigent person money, or paid the rent for a poor mother knows that giving is one of life's greatest joys. God will not deny the poor this joy.

Interestingly, intertwined with the codification of tithing into law, we find this: "Woe to him who puts a poor man to shame!" God forbids us to look upon a poor man with disdain or to raise one's voice to him for his heart is already broken and his spirit crushed. We are to help the poor.

> If there is among you a poor man of your brethren, within any of the gates in your land which the LORD your God is giving you, you shall not harden your heart nor shut your hand from your poor brother, but you shall open your hand wide to him and willingly lend him sufficient for his need, whatever he needs. Beware lest there be a wicked thought in your heart, saying, "The seventh year, the year of release, is at hand," and your eye be evil against your poor brother and you give him nothing, and he cry out to the LORD against you, and it become sin among you. You shall surely give to him, and your heart should not be grieved when you give to him, because for this thing the LORD your God will bless you in all your works and in all to which you put your hand. For the poor will never cease from the land; therefore I command you, saying, "You shall open your hand wide to your brother, to your poor and your needy, in your land." (Deuteronomy 15:7-11).

> ...Then you shall help him, like a stranger or a sojourner, that he may live with you (Leviticus 25:35).

We are to present gifts with sympathy, cheerfully, and with a Christlike attitude.

This far we see that no matter who we are, we are minimally required to tithe; and further, we are "to share [our] resources freely with the poor," and we are to do these things with a warm heart. Learning to tithe and give are integral parts of the sanctification process and every Christian's duty.

We see examples of the principle of giving throughout the Bible. Among the most dedicated to this principle were the earliest Christians. In the book of Acts, we see the first Christians trying to live by these instructions. "Now the multitude of those who believed were of one heart and one soul...but they had all things in common" (Acts 4:32).

Evidence of True Faith. We find a particularly thought provoking commentary on giving in the book James.

> What does it profit, my brethren, if someone says he has faith but does not have works? Can faith save him? If a brother or sister is naked and destitute of daily food, and one of you says to them, "Depart in peace, be warmed and filled," but you do not give them the things which are needed for the body, what does it profit? (James 2:14-16)

Tithing and giving are doing what Christ would do, it is what we would want done to us were we in need.

Generosity and American Christian Heritage

Nowhere does our Christian heritage glow brighter than it does in American's giving to the needy. Examples abound. Internationally, we are always the first in line to help nations in need.

Do Good to Your Enemies. Our country has never hesitated to engage in huge projects such as the Marshall Plan after World War II. The victor did not go in and occupy the defeated lands but sent food, clothing, and massive amounts of economic help to the vanquished. From President Johnson's War on Poverty to our states' unemployment insurance programs, the mark of God's law is upon American giving.

Viet Nam. As a Viet Nam combat veteran, I never witnessed a GI so tired that he would not stop and give a child food or even order clothing from his folks back in America to give a near naked civilian. And soap – the Vietnamese paid more than a day's wages for soap. We gave most of what we were issued to mothers so that they could clean their children properly in that hot sweaty equatorial climate that was the Mekong Delta. Our combat medics spent far more time helping sick and impoverished civilians than they did taking care of soldiers. What other country's army behaves like this?

Disaster Relief. The next time there is a hurricane, earthquake, flood, or peacekeeping mission anywhere in the world, watch Americans rise to the cause. That is our Godly heritage; it is unheard of in human history. No, we have not gotten it right all the time, but our people keep trying to get it right and we keep on giving. If God is rewarding America for anything, it is for our giving.

Righteousness Exalts a Nation. God has blessed us as a nation. When God created the world, He made every person a caretaker, a gardener. For that purpose, God endows each individual with talents and the ability to work to build some kind of wealth. In order to give, we must use what God gives us, be it talent or wealth.

Investing the Lord's Assets

The parable of the three servants illustrates our responsibility in handling the Lord's affairs. In the following parable, contrast the fear of the servant with one talent with the bold obedience of the other two servants. The two faithful servants were willing to take risks for their master. They did his work, used their God-given talents for His glory:

> For the kingdom of heaven is like a man traveling to a far country, who called his own servants and delivered his goods to them. And to one he gave five talents, to another two, and to another one, to each according to his own ability; and immediately he went on a journey. Then he who had received the five talents went and traded with them, and made another five talents. And likewise he who had received two gained two more also. But he who had received one went and dug in the ground, and hid his lord's money. After a long time the lord of those servants came and settled accounts with them.
>
> So he who had received five talents came and brought five other talents, saying, "Lord, you delivered to me five talents; look, I have

gained five more talents besides them." His lord said to him, "Well done, good and faithful servant; you were faithful over a few things, I will make you ruler over many things. Enter into the joy of your lord." He also who had received two talents came and said, "Lord, you delivered to me two talents; look, I have gained two more talents besides them." His lord said to him, "Well done, good and faithful servant; you have been faithful over a few things, I will make you ruler over many things. Enter into the joy of your lord."

Then he who had received the one talent came and said, "Lord, I knew you to be a hard man, reaping where you have not sown, and gathering where you have not scattered seed. And I was afraid, and went and hid your talent in the ground. Look, there you have what is yours."

But his lord answered and said to him, "You wicked and lazy servant, you knew that I reap where I have not sown, and gather where I have not scattered seed. So you ought to have deposited my money with the bankers, and at my coming I would have received back my own with interest. So take the talent from him, and give it to him who has ten talents. 'For to everyone who has, more will be given, and he will have abundance; but from him who does not have, even what he has will be taken away. And cast the unprofitable servant into the outer darkness. There will be weeping and gnashing of teeth'" (Matthew 25:14-30).

Aesop's fable of "The Miser" helps us to understand the "wicked and lazy servant." We read:

> A miser sold all of his property and bought a mass of gold, which he buried in a secret place to which he made frequent visits of inspection. Someone who had noticed his coming and going found the treasure and carried it off, and when the miser returned and discovered his loss, he wailed and tore his hair in a frenzy of grief. Someone who saw him agonizing, after learning the cause, said to him, "Don't grieve, my friend, just take a stone and bury it in the same place and think of it as gold in a vault. Even when the gold was there you made no use of it."

We are to use the talents God gives us to create forms of wealth for His glory or our talents are wasted. This parable certainly emphasizes our opening Scripture from Malachi. If we do not serve God by giving, we are robbing Him of the work He is due, and He will take back what He has given. However, if we do as He directs, He promises to, "open for you the windows of heaven and pour out for you such blessing that there will not be room enough to receive it."

Furthermore, which of the servants lived an exciting life while the master was away? It certainly was not the "wicked and lazy servant." From him we learn that it takes more than good intentions to lead a good life and to please God. Although the "wicked and lazy servant" did not use his master's gold in riotous living or for evil, fear was the guiding factor in his life. And so he just did nothing. Christ said to the church at Laodicea,

> I know your works, that you are neither cold nor hot. I could wish you were cold or hot. So then, because you are lukewarm, and neither cold nor hot, I will vomit you out of My mouth (Revelation 3:15-16).

Many times scholars have emphasized the end-time issues clearly implied by the parable of the three servants and missed the parallel day-by-day message. People who take their life's work seriously do come out ahead of those who just glide though life without taking risks. Often Jesus spoke of the ethical living and social action that must characterize the lives of His disciples. No matter how small or large, we must employ our God-given talents for His glory. We must be responsible caretakers of His gracious endowments. The two faithful servants had to do their master's work. We too are to work. He created us to experience His wonderful plan. Working for God, acting like Christ would act, is realizing that wonder.

Paul says we should give all that we are to serve God:

> I beseech you therefore, brethren, by the mercies of God, that you present your bodies a living sacrifice, holy, acceptable to God, which is your reasonable service. And do not be conformed to this world, but be transformed by the renewing of your mind, that you may prove what is that good and acceptable and perfect will of God (Romans 12:1-2).

James says it differently. "But someone will say, 'You have faith, and I have works.' Show me your faith without your works, and I will show you my faith by my works" (2:18).

"Just Accept Christ." We hear preachers say, "Just accept Christ!" And if that's all a person does, he or she is still dead in their sins and has no spiritual rebirth. Therefore no spiritual fruit can be borne in his or her life. This may very well be one of the root causes why so few professed Christians go on to sanctification, because they have not been born again – they do not have God's spiritual DNA in their souls.

Any person on the street will "accept Christ" as a good man, as a great example, as a great teacher. Even Moslems "accept" Him as a great prophet. But mere acceptance does not save. Neither John the Baptist, Jesus, Paul, Peter nor any other biblical preacher ever preached "accept Christ." They all consistently preached repentance and faith as the essential conditions of salvation. Acceptance does not equal repentance. Repentance and faith are inseparable, both growing out of deep contrition – a godly sorrow for sin which in turn produces long-term fruit in the life of a believer:

> For godly sorrow produces repentance leading to salvation, not to be regretted; but the sorrow of the world produces death. For observe this very thing, that you sorrowed in a godly manner: What diligence it produced in you, what clearing of yourselves, what indignation [against sin], what fear [reverential awe], what vehement desire [to please the Savior], what zeal [to serve God], what vindication [proving their salvation was genuine]! In all things you proved yourselves to be clear in this matter (2 Corinthians 7:10, 11).

Even David understood this when he wrote, "The sacrifices of God are a broken spirit, A broken and a contrite heart – These, O God, You will not despise" (Psalm 51:17).

We do not deny that there is an element of acceptance inherent in repentance, but there is no element of repentance inherent in "accepting Christ."

Going Further. The parable of the three servants takes us far beyond initial salvation. Look at what Paul says in Romans or what James says in his book. God calls us to move on to sanctification. Christianity is a life-long pursuit – not of salvation which is instantaneous and eternal – but of personal godliness. Rewarding Christianity is hard work. Christianity begins with the Holy Spirit convicting and drawing the sinner to repentance and faith, whereupon God responds with regeneration, imparting eternal life, a new creation. But that is only the beginning. Being now made alive unto God, being partaker of the divine nature, we then go onward and upward:

> Likewise you also, reckon yourselves to be dead indeed to sin, but alive

to God in Christ Jesus our Lord. Therefore do not let sin reign in your mortal body, that you should obey it in its lusts. And do not present your members as instruments of unrighteousness to sin, but present yourselves to God as being alive from the dead, and your members as instruments of righteousness to God. For sin shall not have dominion over you, for you are not under law but under grace (Romans 6:11-14).

Listen to Jesus. "Every tree that does not bear good fruit is cut down and thrown into the fire. Therefore by their fruits you will know them. Not everyone who says to Me, 'Lord, Lord,' shall enter the kingdom of heaven, but he who does the will of My Father in heaven" (Matthew 7:19-21).

There is yet another aspect of the principle of giving. The Bible was freely given and is freely taught. The people who dedicate themselves to studying the Bible and following its dictates receive more, while those who neglect the study of the ways and will of the Lord will lose what they have. We Christians often rely too much on prayer alone and not enough on the study of the objective Word and the work of obedience to it.

Some believe that is one reason some Christians and many churches are in decline. The church that does nothing dies. That is the way God has set things up. The more we study the Bible, the more learning takes place, the more Christians work, and the more our lives honor God. The more one has, the more one will receive. The divine issue of justice is not always consistent with human understanding of equitable recompense.

One point of the parable of the three servants is that the person who uses wisely what God has given will receive much more than he or she deserves under the human scheme of things. We must learn as much as possible and work as hard as possible because that is God's will, and that is where our reward is.

The man or woman who knows firsthand the gifts, goodness, and mercy God has given him or her should give with warmth and affection to others. This will be a benefit to them, and, equally important, it is a blessing to God. Yes, a blessing to God. Nothing pleases Him more than for us to join Him in His work.

He looks on our lives in tenderness for He loves us deeply. He has not counted the long years during which His gifts, goodness, and mercy have followed us without slackness. However, He longs to see a measure of those same gifts, goodness, and mercy passed on to others. He wants us to live in His image. He wants all able-bodied men and women to act toward others as He has acted toward us. That is joining Him in His work. That is loving God. He longs to see that love. Then God is satisfied.

Regardless of our occupation, when we work hard and righteously, it is as if we are bringing our treasure, the offering of our lives and the fruits of our labors, into God's house. That is proclaiming His glory. We are to work – to till, subdue, and have godly dominion over the earth God has entrusted to us. Our witness, our lives, the way we live, and the examples we set, are the greatest instruments to bring people to Christ. God wants us to subdue the world and turn it back into the Garden of Eden He intended and created at the beginning. If we are truly Christian, if we are enjoying what God has given us, if we are working hard, we are accomplishing more than we know.

What about you? Are you personally participating fully in the joy that goes with giving of yourself and your wealth? Try it. See if God will not "open for you the windows of heaven and pour out for you such blessing that there will not be room enough to receive it." These are not the kinds of blessings that "moth and rust doth corrupt, and thieves break through and steal." These are blessing that you will treasure.

11 : Your Heritage

"If you keep on doing what you've always done, you're going to keep getting what you always got!"
—Earl Nightingale

This book presents the heritage of an American family. The book gives our children an opportunity to know more than the name of one of their ancestors. Like many American families, our family valued religious freedom enough to leave their native England and move to primitive Massachusetts in the early 1600's. Our ancestors came to Massachusetts imbibed with the idea that they were people under God. Our family hated serfdom enough to leave their native Scotland and move to North Carolina in the 1750's. Our ancestors came to North Carolina knowing that they were created in God's image, and not subservient to any human being. This is our Christian heritage.

Because of this same kind of heritage, most Americans believe in God. But there is more. Our family's heritage is walking on life's narrow path, seeking sanctification. Our heritage replaces "believe in God" with "believes God." This book attempts to explain this transition.

Personal Sanctification: A Rare Subject Today

We started this book with grace and quickly emphasized the need to study the Bible, particularly the Ten Commandments and the other 603 laws in the Pentateuch. Paul tells us that this is necessary so that we will know how sinful we are, how hurtful to our own happiness we are. Then we discussed our role model, Jesus, who did a work that writes His laws on our hearts. He preached, exemplified, and lived an attitude whereby our attitudes are tuned with His and our conduct becomes godly.

Jesus must be our role model for, quoting one of my mother's favorite American poems:

> The gods we worship write their names on our faces, be sure of that. And we will worship something – have no doubt of that either. We may think that our tribute is paid in secret in the dark recesses of the heart – but it is out. That which dominates our imagination and our thoughts will determine our life and character. Therefore it behooves us to be careful what we are worshipping, for what we are worshipping we are becoming.
>
> —Ralph Waldo Emerson

Are we attempting to become like Jesus? He was humble and yet intrepid. He was meek and yet fearless. He believed and practiced an ideal: the noblest duty in life is the promotion of happiness and the welfare of others.

Self-discipline is basic to this noble idea. We must learn to deny ourselves. We practice the humility of Jesus by subordinating ourselves to the welfare of others. We must struggle to do what we ought versus following our own desires. This goes against modern philosophy, but this is Christianity.

Think here of the quote used from Thomas A'Kempis' *Imitation of Christ:*

> The teachings of Christ far transcend all the teachings of the saints,

and who-so-ever has His spirit will discover, concealed in it, heavenly manna. But many people, although they often hear the Gospel, feel little desire to follow it....

Plainly, many people never embrace sanctification.

Our talents are different than are Christ's. We are each endowed with certain unique abilities that are designed to fit perfectly into the body of Christ, His church and His earth. Indeed, we are to use these talents to serve others, bringing them to Christ, preparing the earth for His return.

Thy Will be Done on Earth. Jesus taught us to pray, "Thy kingdom come, Thy will be done." Jesus asked us to join Him in making this world into the Garden of Eden that God intended for it to be when He created the world. Jesus tells us to ask God, our Father and only utterly paramount ruler of the universe, to come and establish His sovereignty in our hearts and eventually in the hearts of all people on the earth.

This attitude recognizes the formidable conflict between His divine sovereignty and our self-willed ego. When we pray our Lord's Prayer, we are praying that His kingdom come. We are saying that we will allow God, by His indwelling Spirit, to decide for us the work in which we shall join Him and how we shall live our lives. Our actions will then be like those of Christ.

When Christ said, "Thy kingdom come," He envisioned His own kingdom on earth. He envisioned the Spirit of God coming into our heart at regeneration and justification, to make His habitation in us. Because we are created in God's image, He gave us our independence. However, we soon find that we cannot bear life on our own. We were not created to do that. Jesus did not model independence but dependence. This dependency is necessary if we are to grow to the perfection necessary to live with God in that perfect place called heaven. Jesus pictured God's attitude as permeating and invading the whole of our lives – that His authority would be totally established in each mind and will. His kingdom is within us.

If the kingdom of God is within us, then we will make it our business to see that nothing enters to harm or offend His sovereignty. From what we eat to our thoughts, goals, and actions in life, we will permit neither gluttony, drunkenness, nor drugs to harm our temple.

We will apply the same practices to our minds that we do to our bodies, carefully replacing, for example, the violence and sex of television and movies with Bible study and church work. We will permit no subversive material into our minds, emotions or wills. Then, as sanctified Christians, we are better able to witness, to help make this world into the paradise God intended.

Paul on Sanctification. Next, this book moves from Christ's example to Paul's understanding of sanctification. Paul presents an overview of the single most essential tool in a Christian's armor: prayer. Not just prayer, but prayer to help in the sanctification process. This kind of prayer is not selfish or self-serving; this kind of prayer serves others.

But mainly the typical format of the Pauline epistles consists of presenting the heavy doctrinal principles that underlie God's nature and our salvation. Then he follows in each epistle with a section on sanctification. In this way he says in effect: "Now in light of these great doctrinal principles, here is how we are to behave."

Contemporary Issues. Then we discuss a number of contemporary issues explaining what the Bible says about each. We study the law, again as Paul explains, so that we will know what sin is. For as Christians on the road to sanctification, until the law is written in our minds as well as on our hearts, we must know what habits we are to forsake via the love of Jesus, and what practices to put in their place.

Renouncing those contemporary sins requires a forgiving spirit, the knowledge that God has forgiven us, and that God offers that same forgiveness to all. We are not to hate those who have sinned against us, even as Christ did not hate those who crucified Him. He had only pity for those who sinned against Him and held no grudge against them. Rather, Jesus invited them to join Him just as on the road to Damascus He invited Saul of Tarsus, the predator of Christians, to be Paul the Apostle. We are to show sinners the way by loving them.

God Calls us to Give. Then there is giving, not just our money, but also our all. As Paul said, make your life a living sacrifice. That is our duty.

Being a living sacrifice means, among other things, that we study the Bible. The Bible is where we gain an understanding of human nature. This understanding tells us that people make mistakes. We should expect that. Our challenge is to succeed, in spite of the failures of our fellow human beings and in spite of our own human frailty, and to succeed in the most loving way we can. The Bible tells us that vice, however tempting, invites neither reward nor respect – neither self-respect nor respect from others. Indeed, the Bible teaches that self-respect is, in truth, fear of God.

Seeking Wisdom. When we are unsure of our duty, we must seek not only the wisdom in the Bible but also the advice of older and wiser persons. We must listen to those who share our vision. We must share our concerns and problems with those we trust. We must ask their opinion. Then we must make our decision. We are not to fear failure. But if we fail, we must never blame those who advised us. Denying our own ego, we should never needlessly remind someone of a failure or a wrong they did. When others fail, forgiveness should be swift and complete. Our loved ones need us most when they let us down. There is much white lying today because there is little forgiveness. We must renounce our pride.

The commandment to be a living sacrifice brings to mind a question a career advisor asked me just before I graduated from college: "How can you make your life successful?" The advisor went on to say that I must first define what I considered success to be. Every Christian needs to confront this question.

Many people today define success in terms of pleasure, amusement, sex, and fun – not too mature. Others define success in terms of wealth, power, and prestige – totally worldly. While a Christian's definition of success may include being reasonably happy here on earth, that is not the goal of a Christian's life. The goal is growth in character, in Christlikeness. The goal includes serving others. The goal considers our God-given talents as well as the material gifts God has blessed us with.

God's rule: to whom much is given, of him much is expected. The thoughtful manner in which we never abuse an advantage we have over another is a mark of a Christian. We should never feel haughty because of some vice we do not have in common with another person. We must maintain a sense of humility even when there are no current circumstances that do it for us. Pride is such a foolish habit. Never consider anyone more susceptible to error than we ourselves are. We never know how long it will be before we make a moral slip.

The Impressions We Make! Remember, God wants to be a part of all our actions. Recently, while driving down an interstate, I saw two vans and three automobiles pass our car, all moving at high speed. The vans and automobiles were full of young people and read "First Baptist Church" on their sides. Two of the cars had Christian symbols on the back, and the third had a minister's sign on its back. Would you want your children riding with these men? Do these men wonder why they do not have more kids on their church trips? These drivers did not have enough discipline to drive the speed limit even when transporting life's most precious cargo. If Christ is in our life, we will let Him influence all facets of our behavior.

The Holy Spirit Within

In the Old Testament, God resided in the temple. Now people are the temple (I Corinthians 3:16). Why? Because Jesus sent something more powerful to dwell within us:

> Nevertheless I tell you the truth. It is to your advantage that I go away; for if I do not go away, the Helper will not come to you; but if I depart, I will send Him to you.... However, when He, the Spirit of truth, has come, He will guide you into all truth; for He will not speak on His own authority, but whatever He hears He will speak; and He will tell you things to come. He will glorify Me, for He will take of what is Mine and declare it to you. All things that the Father has are Mine. Therefore I said that He will take of Mine and declare it to you (John 16:7, 13-15).

Paul said, "He who has begun a good work in you will complete it until the day of Jesus Christ" (Philippians 1:6). We must realize that we can trust the growth process no matter how we feel while in the midst of it. Because of the Holy Spirit, we can stop worrying about whether or not our relationship is secure and get on with the work of growth.

We Are Not Alone. The Holy Spirit is not a formula or a method but a person. Our job is to ask the Spirit to be in our lives to help us join God in His work.

> So I say to you: Ask and it will be given to you; seek and you will find; knock and the door will be opened to you. For everyone who asks receives; he who seeks finds; and to him who knocks, the door will be opened.
>
> If a son asks for bread from any father among you, will he give him a stone? Or if he asks for a fish, will he give him a serpent instead of a fish? Or if he asks for an egg, will he offer him a scorpion? If you then, being evil, know how to give good gifts to your children, how much more will your heavenly Father give the Holy Spirit to those who ask Him (Luke 11:9-13).

We are not alone. God wants us to be dependent on Him. The Holy Spirit will lead us away from what is destructive and turn us to do what is good, the things Jesus would do.

> However, when He, the Spirit of truth, has come, He will guide you into all truth… (John 16:13).
>
> Now to Him who is able to do exceedingly abundantly above all that we ask or think, according to the power that works in us…be glory in the church by Christ Jesus.… (Ephesians 3:20).

Within our limited capacity, our job is to yield to the Spirit and allow Him to have control.

This new life will not remove the pain or struggle from us anymore than God lifted pain from Jesus. Neither will we find ourselves free from sin. Indeed, we will begin to see more and more clearly just how sinful we are. Neither will sanctification be instantaneous. Paul did not yield, we must also keep working (see Philippians 3:12-13). Peter said that good character is built over time in ever-increasing measure (II Peter 1:8). We will be made "new" but not yet "complete" (II Corinthians 5:17). However, we are "being sanctified" (Hebrews 10:14).

Jesus promised "the kingdom of heaven" to those who were poor in spirit (Matthew 5:3). So constantly remember the parable of the Pharisee and the tax collector (Luke 18:9-14) and Paul's personal anguish over his inability to do the right thing (Romans 7:15-24). Such feelings are the feelings of one who is growing. Such feelings are the feelings of being cured of narcissism, self-righteousness, and all other problems of character.

An Ever-present Helper. The Holy Spirit is not with us to make us feel better but rather to help us grow. "To him who is afflicted, kindness should be shown by his friend, Even though he forsakes the fear of the Almighty" (Job 6:14). Being aware of our spiritual poverty, our incompleteness, orients us toward God and His ways. He sent His Holy Spirit to repair and grow us. This most probably will take time. Do not despair but understand the wonderful growth that is carrying us on to perfection.

"Assuredly, I say to you, whoever does not receive the kingdom of God as a little child will by no means enter it" (Mark 10:15). Children by nature are relationship oriented. When they hurt or fear they immediately reach for a comforting parent. We are spiritual babes (I Peter 2:2). Sanctification makes us reach for our Father and ultimately join Him.

This old soldier knows that a drill instructor never asked a private to understand why he or she needs to learn discipline and how to behave in combat. A drill instructor says do it this way or else. No choice is given. They know what a soldier should do in combat and they are going to train soldiers to behave that way whether or not that person understands why. Later, in actual combat, soldiers are glad their drill instructors did what they did.

Paul said we are to put on the whole amour of God. That amour is acting in accord with God's laws. The amour works whether or not we understand why. It is having the amour on that protects us, and not our understanding why. So be not dissuaded by those who do not understand Christianity. Do not succumb to their wanting us to convince them we are doing something of which they approve.

God wants us to have understanding, to develop wisdom. After we have studied God's laws and disciplined ourselves to obey His laws, after we have put God's ways into practice, slowly by living in that mode we will develop wisdom. And, as in the parable of the three servants, the more we have, the more we will receive. We will receive much more than we deserve under any earthly scheme. God acts that way.

Make the Effort: Try

On one of our family's ancient crests is a motto that has stuck with me since I first read it as a teenager. The motto said, "To be rather than to seem." In an age when Hollywood stars and public figures spend large amounts of money painting images, often false images, of themselves; in an age when politicians use focus groups to tell them what they are supposed to believe and how they are to act, this ancient bit of wisdom is valuable if unpopular. Nevertheless, it is a Christian attitude – make the effort.

We must learn as much as possible, work as hard as possible, because that is where our reward is. That is God's will, His design. Our inheritance: go and study, go and obey, go and work. Let God handle the rest. We have the word of our Father, God Almighty, that if we do as He asks, life will be rewarding and rewarded.

Written for my children and my children's children, this book may cause you to ask, "How good a life did old Dad lead?" While you may be looking to old Dad for perfection, this author says with no satisfaction, you will have to settle for less.

You will find that Dad has not led a perfect life, not by a long shot. But he tried. Make the effort; that is the message: try! Try sanctification. It is difficult, but the reward is in joining God in His work. What happens between you and God will be your heritage. Try!

www.ingramcontent.com/pod-product-compliance
Lightning Source LLC
Chambersburg PA
CBHW031249290426
44109CB00012B/501